Happy Witch

ACTIVITIES, SPELLS, AND RITUALS TO CALM THE CHAOS AND FIND YOUR JOY

Mandi Em

Author of *Witchcraft Therapy*

ADAMS MEDIA

NEW YORK   LONDON   TORONTO   SYDNEY   NEW DELHI

Adams Media
An Imprint of Simon & Schuster, Inc.
100 Technology Center Drive
Stoughton, Massachusetts 02072

First Adams Media hardcover edition October 2022

ADAMS MEDIA and colophon are trademarks of Simon & Schuster.

For information about special discounts for bulk purchases, please contact Simon & Schuster Special Sales at 1-866-506-1949 or business@simonandschuster.com.

The Simon & Schuster Speakers Bureau can bring authors to your live event. For more information or to book an event contact the Simon & Schuster Speakers Bureau at 1-866-248-3049 or visit our website at www.simonspeakers.com.

Interior design by Sylvia McArdle
Interior images © Etsy.com/DigitalCurio, MinimalMarks, LaRoseArtStudios

Manufactured in the United States of America

1 2022

Library of Congress Cataloging-in-Publication Data has been applied for.

ISBN 978-1-5072-1971-3
ISBN 978-1-5072-1972-0 (ebook)

DEDICATION

Dedicated to every obstacle
that was secretly hiding an open door.

CONTENTS

CHAPTER 6

Be Soulful ... 189

INTRODUCTION

At its core, witchcraft is a source of empowerment, where anyone, regardless of age, spirituality, or *whatever* can tease out happiness through performance, play, following impulse, and inviting some magical joy into their lives. Beyond just spell jars and candle magic, there's a whole world of magical ways to conjure up a little childlike wonder and healing to infuse joy into your daily witchcraft practice. By approaching your craft as a divine tool for wellness and growth, you can bust open the doors to happiness and healing, every day!

Happy Witch provides a road map for conjuring up your best high-vibe life in a world that can often have you feeling depleted and as though you're asleep at the wheel. You'll find practical tools and advice on tackling the messy work of meeting yourself where you're at and making big shifts in order to cultivate a life that's full of magical joy.

Each chapter that follows captures an element of *being* that leads to *thriving*. This book will cover how to use witchcraft to:

- **Be Free** by laying the groundwork for a magically empowered mindset.
- **Be Wild** by connecting with nature and leaning into rewilding as a source of joy.
- **Be Playful** by inviting play and creativity into your life through spells and rituals designed to heal and delight your inner child.
- **Be Still** by unearthing bliss in the quieter work of your witchy practices, exploring your shadows to find the light.
- **Be Connected** by using relational magic to enjoy your connections with yourself and others on a deeper level.
- **Be Soulful** by embodying the magic you want to see in the world.

Each of the fifty entries divided among these chapters explores one way that witchcraft can help you flourish into the happy, self-empowered witch you deserve to be. You'll uncover the roadblocks that can pop up and mess with your vibe, and find simple spells, rituals, and other magical activities for reclaiming happiness regardless of what life throws at you. After all, cultivating a life that's juicy, delicious, and ripe with joy is not only #goals—it's your divine birthright! So are you ready to step up and invoke the badass happy witch inside of you?

MAGICAL BASICS

Although the term "witchcraft" can conjure up images of edgy aesthetics and devilishly compelling fictional characters, the reality is that it is a healing modality that has the power to transform your life! Witchcraft is a practice, and one that can help you connect more deeply with yourself, with nature, and with the larger mysteries of the Universe. Best of all, witchcraft allows you to pick up the reins of your own life, directing each day to be an adventure in joy, healing, and self-growth. How exactly? Through its transformative nature. We witches are shape-shifters who refuse to be governed by limiting beliefs about what is true and possible. Instead, we seek to break open the doors of possibility and transmute pain into peace through shadow work, ritual, spells, and spiritual self-care practices. While the mundane dimension of experience can be full of stressors and drama, magic allows us to tap in to joy and align with happiness. Though every witch's particular craft will look different, for most, this course in personal power through positive magic is at the heart of their work.

In the next sections, you will explore essential elements of magic. But, before we get into that, it's important to understand that while magic is a powerful tool, it is not a catch-all quick fix. All magical workings must be matched by real-world efforts for best results. This means real mundane action, as well as digging into your belief systems and making sure that you are making yourself available for the outcomes you want. For example, as a response to toxic positivity (the bypassing of truly feeling and honoring your emotions in favor of "just thinking happy thoughts!"—bleh!) in the spiritual world, there's been an attitude shift and wariness toward the topic of adopting a brighter outlook. However, in some cases, this has been overcorrected to the point that it can leave people feeling jaded and salty about cultivating a brighter mindset.

Balance and perspective are key—especially in conversations about happiness and joy, where circumstances and injustice can make the playing field pretty imbalanced. You need to simultaneously hold space for that, while recognizing the immense power you have as an individual to connect with the joyous wellspring within. Joy can be a powerful act of sovereign rebellion against the systems and contexts that can make life feel draining and out of your control at times!

Essential Techniques

Given that every witch's practice is so unique, there are very few "rules" (if any) when it comes to practicing the craft. That being said, there are some magical basics that lay the foundation for getting best results. The following sections outline these basics and define concepts that will help you get the most from this book.

Just a little note on safety and protection before you start: Prior to doing witchcraft, there are precautions you can take in order to keep yourself both physically and energetically safe. Practices such as smoke cleansing or circle-casting can be utilized to keep you and your workings safe in the energetic sense, while proper fire safety while using candles and such during a ritual, spell, or other technique can keep your body and property safe. (Shout-out to my fellow fire hazard witches!) Additionally, although the craft can be used as a powerful wellness tool, it is not a substitution for professional physical or mental healthcare, should you need it. Your safety and well-being are very important parts of your magic!

Energy Work

In witchcraft, the practitioner raises their energy in order to propel their spells and rituals, making energy work a pretty crucial technique for getting the most from your craft! Energy work is the practice of sensing and working with the energies both within and outside of yourself. Although this can sound a little "out there" to the uninitiated, most people, witches or not, have some experience sensing and/or working with energies in mundane life. For example, the electric sensation that can come before a kiss, or the heavy sensation that lingers in a room where people have been arguing. Even historical sites with a rich backstory can carry a particular "vibe" that even the most skeptical person can perceive. This is a dimension of experience that you can sense, even if you don't yet have a mundane explanation for it. Since witches essentially have one foot in the mundane and the other in the realm of the mystic, they are able to work with and manipulate these energies for specific purposes.

Additionally, everyone has an energetic field of their own. When you hear about "vibes" in witchcraft, this refers to the idea that, because we are energetic beings, everyone's energetic field carries certain vibrational frequencies that are in a constant state of flux depending on environment, emotions, interactions, etc. Happier, more elevated states correspond with a higher vibrational frequency, and lower base emotions such as anger and fear carry a more dense and heavy vibrational frequency. Through aligning your energy to higher and more positive frequencies, you are able to attract more positive things and experiences. This is why dancing to your favorite upbeat song can shift your mood in a big way, and why dwelling in the negative can keep you from seeing your own blessings.

Cleansing and Opening Magical Spaces

Magical workings require magical states of consciousness. These are mental and energetic zones that you don't typically dip into while doing mundane things like shopping for paper towels. For most witches, ritual and spellwork are preceded by certain actions and behaviors to prepare for magic, such as cleansing and opening up magical spaces. Engaging in these actions makes it so that not only is your space prepped for magical workings, but so are your brain and your vibes!

Cleansing is a technique where the practitioner takes responsibility to clear the energy of a space, of tools, or even of themselves prior to performing witchcraft. There are a variety of ways to cleanse, one of the most recognizable ways being smoke cleansing. Smoke cleansing typically involves using bundles of smoking herbs or incense to clear objects, people, or spaces, with a particular intention. Sometimes the intention is simply to clear out harmful or unwanted energies, while other times the intention is to cleanse in order to prepare for magical workings.

Opening up magical space can look very different from witch to witch, and even from spell to spell. Some witches cast circles, creating an energetic zone of magic and protection for ritual and spellwork, while others may call on elements, directional corners, or even spirits to help set up and protect a space for magic. It really does depend on the intentions and worldview of the witch. For many of us chaos witches, this process might look a little less formal than what you'd expect based on the prevailing aesthetics of modern spirituality, but it is effective nonetheless! The important thing is to lean into your intuition and trust your inner guidance to open up magical space in a way (or multiple ways) that feels right for you and your practice.

Grounding and Centering

Many people roam through life on autopilot, with their energies scattered and their minds and bodies in a state of disconnection. This clearly is not the most effective headspace for getting into a potent magical zone! Grounding and centering is the practice of controlling and calming your personal energy and integrating the mind, body, and spirit. It allows you to pause, regroup your energies, and focus your will in accordance with your intent. Grounding and centering is commonly done by witches pre- and post- ritual or spellwork in order to focus their energies in a way that supports their magical workings.

Although there are many methods of grounding and centering that you can draw on, the most impactful ways to ground yourself involve anchoring yourself in the moment directly through your physical awareness, such as by standing with your bare feet on the dirt or grass, practicing mindful breathing, or tuning in to sensory experiences, leaning into what you can hear or taste in that moment. Methods that utilize nature, such as meditating outdoors, lying on the ground, or sinking your feet into the sand, are especially powerful. With all methods, the goal is to pull your energy and awareness out of the overthinky brain vortex and back into your body in a deliberate and connected way.

Spellcrafting

Spellcrafting is the act of formulating and casting spells to achieve a specific desired outcome. You can get wonderful tried and tested spells from books (like this one!). However, magical practitioners also have the option to craft their own spells once they feel comfortable and adept at doing so. When crafting a spell, it's important to get very specific with your intentions, then choose ingredients and/or elements that support those objectives. That being said, I am a huge advocate for the practitioner being the most essential component of magic: *You are the spell!* Don't underestimate the power of your own intuition and inner guidance to help you in crafting magical practices that will have particularly potent power and meaning for you. Much of your practice can be experimental and an opportunity to play and carve out your own unique path, guided by your intuition. This is very meaningful, considering that personal belief plays such an effective role in witchcraft.

Witches and their magic existed long before there were online retailers or local metaphysical shops. So if you find yourself in the position of missing a certain ingredient for a spell, never fear! A solid foundation of self-knowledge and skill with harnessing your own energy will always be an effective substitution.

Once the intent, ingredients, and methodology of the spell have been sorted, the magical practitioner raises their energy to essentially "give life" to the spell, propelling the intention to manifest in reality. This is the spark of magic in the spellcrafting that transforms desire and ingredients into noticeable shifts in the real world—very akin to the concept of manifesting (more on this next).

Manifesting

The basic philosophy of manifesting is that, as a conscious being, you have the power to cocreate your reality by adjusting your own thoughts, energy, and belief systems, aligning yourself to the outcome that you desire. Although this concept has been around since ancient times, it reemerged in the mainstream with the New Thought movement and continues to be popular in spiritual circles today (particularly Law of Attraction, Law of Assumption, and Law of Belief). Many witches and spiritual types are well versed in using the principles of manifesting as a catalyst to shift inner and outer reality, making life a mutable experience in which *you* direct the story!

With any discussions of manifesting, it's important to note that you should be cautious to not get yourself into a position where your beliefs can negatively impact your wellness, experience, or self-concept. For example, a person with anxiety and intrusive thoughts shouldn't buy into the idea that *all* thoughts create reality or that physical illnesses are a result of "bad vibes" or whatever other nonsense. This is just more of the kind of toxic BS that gives modern spirituality a bad reputation. Some thoughts are just that: thoughts. And illness can occur independent of your vibes. That being said, don't underestimate the incredible power you *do* have to guide your reality in the direction you want. This isn't purely a metaphysical concept, either: Many scientific studies back up the principles of mind over matter. As always, the key is balance. The Universe is a space of wonder and chaos! Some things can be intentionally brought into your reality, and some things happen a certain way regardless of how hard you may try to manifest the opposite.

Meditation

Meditation is a mental and physical practice that can be used to deepen the connection with the self, as well as promote relaxation and a whole host of other physical and mental health benefits. Through meditation, you bypass the typical brain chatter to access deeper states of mindfulness by narrowing your focus in a concentrated way. Witches are keen on self-mastery as a tool for growth and wellness, and meditation can help you get there. It lends your workings and practice more potency. Human brains have a real knack for killing the vibe with their overthinky BS, and meditation can help you quiet that shit so that you can access deeper states of knowledge and healing.

There are different methods and approaches to meditation. Focusing on breath, sounds (such as with sound bowl meditations), movement, visualization, etc. are all valid and effective meditation techniques. Although there's a common idea that meditation is about "thinking nothing," the truth is that it is simply about heightening your awareness of the present moment in such a way that you don't get carried off into oblivion by your own thoughts. There is an emphasis on experiencing each moment, releasing it, and moving on to the next, rather than getting caught up in the typical future fretting or dwelling on the past. Thoughts are not the enemy—latching on to them and allowing them to spiral out of control is!

Ritual

Rituals can be hard to define, but to put it simply, they are a set of behaviors or practices that can be performed and repeated over time. For example, blowing out birthday candles and making a wish is a ritual, as is checking your pockets before you leave the house to be sure you have everything. Ritual is a big part of witchcraft, and the level of seriousness can vary, with some rituals being more solemn and ceremonial and others being mundane or even playful in nature.

Some practitioners catch a vibe from performing ceremonial practices such as the Lesser Banishing Ritual of the Pentagram, while others are more into casual chaos-craft such as tossing some salt around and demanding that fates be changed. It's all relative and deeply personal. Feel free to explore what works for you!

Rituals can help you feel more empowered, and in some cases, they can establish a vibe to allow you to slip into a mystical state for your magical work. By inviting more ritual into your life, you are able to hack the mundane, making your reality a more connected and magical experience.

Shadow Work

Shadow work is one of the cornerstones of a witch's personal practice; love and light can only get you so far! Shadow work is about diving into the deeper, hidden parts of yourself in order to heal, remove blocks, and better understand yourself. Through shadow work, you tease out limiting beliefs, spot where your maladaptive tendencies come from, and find the roots to your more pervasive problems and pain. Although shadow work can seem intimidating (it's not exactly comfortable to confront the parts of yourself that your ego has hidden from others), it is imperative for your development as a person and a witch. You need to integrate and understand these parts of yourself in order to keep them from sabotaging you and your magic.

Shadow work can be approached in various ways. Although journaling and meditating on your triggers are a couple of prevailing methods for self-understanding, there is a lot of shadow work that can be done on the fly just by participating in your own life. For instance, examining your triggers and emotional reactions as you move through your day and trying to suss out where these come from and why. Additionally, doing things that challenge you and create immense discomfort is shadow work in action that can heal you while building a new foundation of resilience. Self-awareness, reflection, and viewing your reactions as reflective of the unhealed wounds inside are key.

Just as precious minerals can be mined from the darkness and the muck, so too can you find immense value in the dark corners of your shadows!

Craft a Life You'll Love

Now that you've explored these magical basics, it's time to move forward on the path to empowered positivity! Witchcraft is not only a tool for healing but can also be your companion for crafting a more joyful, inspired life. In the following pages, you will uncover more about how happiness and joy aren't off-limits even though experience and circumstance can give that illusion. Instead, they are threads in the very tapestry of life itself, and they can be conjured up through creativity, play, and honoring your untamed nature. So let's get up off the crossroads and head off on the path to calming the chaos and finding your joy!

CHAPTER 1

Be Free

At the end of the day, we all want to be happy. There's not really a more fundamental goal than this. The dangling potential for happiness motivates us into social relationships and recreational activities and into working for the things that we think will get us there. However, in the chaos of juggling all that stuff, we can lose the plot, neglecting to make space daily for its presence. Happiness is a noble goal, but the first step to conjuring up joy is to actually be open to it as a possibility. This can require taking a sledgehammer to your belief systems.

See, in the modern madness of the human experience, people have a tendency to view happiness as being gated off somewhere beyond reach. This could not be further from the truth! If you assume a door to be locked, you may walk past it for years without ever bothering to jiggle the handle. But what if the door was unlocked the whole time? What if the only thing stopping you from accessing it was your own *belief* that it was off-limits? In this chapter you will use witchcraft to challenge the belief systems that keep happiness on the periphery of your life, and lay the foundations for calling it in. It's time to summon up your magic in order to uncover your own keys to happiness, learn how to become a vibrational match for joy, and push past the BS that would have you feeling disempowered and afraid.

Define Your Happy

So you wanna be happy.

"Happy" is one of those slippery, shape-shifting terms. The word somehow manages to be as two-dimensional and basic as the word "nice," yet it contains multitudes in its simplicity. It's joy, it's contentment, it's pleasure. It's positive feelings and satisfaction. It's the great goal of life, often mistaken for the finish line. In fact, despite attempts to pin it onto some "thing" far off in the future, it's well within your grasp at any given point. Its energy is as present to be conjured up in the dusty corners of rock bottom as it is in some mansion high up in the hills. This is because it lies in your brain, fully independent of context and setting.

What a dreadfully empowering thought!

Any quest to understand, recognize, or seek a thing *must* include a clear and concise definition of *what the thing is*. Like many lofty "I wish I were ____" statements, happiness remains elusive when you neglect to give it form. In the context of science, for example, broad concepts are given shape with finely tuned operational definitions. Meaning, you must *define the thing* in order to *know the thing*, to *measure the thing*, or even to *recognize the thing* in the first place! So I ask you, witch, what does "happy" mean to you? What qualities does it have? What does it look like? What does it feel like? Would you know its presence if it were lurking right behind you?

The broad definition of happiness is subjective well-being. However, what this looks like on an individual level can vary considerably. This is why the task of sorting out what this means and looks like *for you* is so important. Think of your life as the "spell," and your definition of happiness as providing the "ingredients" for that spell. Happiness is as wholly unique as you are!

Defining happiness also helps you glean insight into what it is *not*. When you shine a light on your internal ideas of what happiness is, you illuminate a ton of shadows. This is *necessary*. It's important to know what obstacles lurk within. What traumas pop up on this path? What limits have you placed upon your own head that make the path more burdensome? Is "happy" a trigger? Does it feel safe?

Conversations of happiness and shifting to the positive can be hindered by the very real urge to place judgments upon your own traumas and lurking shadows. However, to truly seek joy in life is to reclaim the multidimensional nature of the concept. There is light in the dark, and dark in the light. Rather than viewing "happy" as this faraway, generic thing that doesn't tell you anything at all, you give it teeth and a space in the present by recognizing it for what it is: a rebellion through joy, pleasure, and play that is always available. It is medicine for the modern-day standard of overwhelm and responsibility. It is a fundamental dimension of the human experience.

So what does happiness mean to you? Use the following ritual to define that shit, and let this working definition act as a guide for how to identify it, pursue it, and feel it!

A Ritual to Define Your Happy

This ritual will help you craft a vision of what happiness looks and feels like to you. After all, the clearer you are on this, the easier time you will have in finding and holding on to it!

Materials

- A notebook or journal and a writing instrument such as a pen or pencil

- Some digital images that represent "happy" for you

- Optional: Incense, cleansing tools of your choice (incense, herbs to burn), crystals, etc.

Start by sitting in a safe, comfortable space. Set the vibe in a way that feels good: Play some calming music (it's best if there are no lyrics, for distractibility's sake), diffuse some pleasant scents, wrap yourself in textured blankets, etc. Feel free to use a cleansing or protective method of your choice (for example, using crystals, smoke cleansing, or casting a circle of protection), as seeking happiness can bring up some shadows (the parts of you that may be repressed or hidden). Crystals may also be used to set the tone.

In your notebook, explore the following questions:

- What does happiness mean to you? What's the operational definition?

- Up until now, have you believed it was attainable? Why or why not?

- Think of a specific time when you were happy. What did that happiness look like? How did it feel?

- What does the happiest version of you look like? How do they respond to triggers? How do they feel? What do they believe to be true?

Now for a manifesting mood board: Collect as many images that scream "happy" to you as you decide (5–10 work well). It is *very important* not to overthink this step! This isn't the SATs. You will not be graded, nor forced to explain your choices. Just pick images that stand out, and assemble them together as either a single collage (a photo grid app or Canva works well for this) or as a gallery in your phone. Look at your mood board regularly to help you keep sight of what happiness means for you and tap in to a space of inviting happiness to you every day.

The caveat? Because it's a subjective state of being, your idea of what happy is will constantly evolve, just as you do. Even when you have done this ritual, you may find that somewhere down the line your definition changes. Simply do this ritual again! If your smartphone is subject to constant upgrades, shouldn't your wellness be as well?

Recognize the Rules That Were Meant for Breaking

When mulling over the most pervasive barriers to living joyfully, the obvious answer is the modern cultural climate. Injustices, social media comparisons, and work-yourself-into-the-groundism can make you feel overwhelmed and pessimistic—an understandable result. However, if all that stuff were cleared away, many would find themselves still unhappy. This is because there's some much-needed housecleaning in the mindset department that needs to occur to clear the way for you to get there. The good news is that this can be tackled no matter what's going on in the world around you!

Everyone has implicit rules and expectations that they hold and use to govern themselves and their behavior. These can act as invisible cages that can restrict the expression of unique magic. Some of these are handed down through societal direction, while others are picked up along the path of your individual life experience. Whether or not you are aware of them, they exist, and they act as guidelines for how to act. However, they go beyond just providing boundaries for how you move through the world. In many cases, they can also obstruct your ability to see what is available and possible for you. The same invisible bars that are designed to keep bad things out can also be a barrier for good things trying to come in.

It's time to harness your inner magic to break free, dear witch!

Some of these rules were meant to be broken: Your expansion as a person may rely on it! The path of the witch is often paved by doing this sort of mindset work, because it's fundamental to living a magically empowered life. It's important for you to come to terms with the fact that you were never really beholden to these limits in the first place; you simply believed you were, as other people believe they are. There's a good chance you may not even vibe with these assumptions or guidelines at all. You may just find that, under close scrutiny, these beliefs are pure BS.

There's really nothing concrete stopping any of us from wearing loud outfits, dancing in the streets, or slathering ourselves in mayo (if that's what you're into). The thing that makes you second-guess acting on your desires in most cases is simply the fear of what could happen next.

Well, here's the thing: It is possible there will be judgment from others. However, these things typically become way bigger and scarier in our imaginations than they are in real life. Mentally, as you continue to imagine negative possibilities that might never happen, you experience them over and over in your mind—without reaping the rewards of having actually *done the thing*. This is what makes your mind so powerful, and this is why self-mastery is such an important skill, especially for the witch.

The uncaged mind recognizes that the urge to conform to limitations or live to please others doesn't deserve space in your brain. To bust open the doors of these invisible cages is to examine every belief you have about happiness and what is possible and ask a simple question: "Is this true because it's actually true, or because I assume it to be?" If following these implicit rules is getting in the way of your wellness and joy, consider whether it's really worth it (Hint: It probably isn't), and then use the following ritual to call in a little rebellious rule-breaking.

A Ritual to Bust Out of Your Cage

It's time to invoke your inner badass witch to bust out of the confines built up in your own mind. As you go through this ritual, remember the following:

- You are worthy of an unlimited life that is dictated by *you*.

- Your living in a way that makes you feel happy and free is your own business. If other people don't like it, that's *their* own business.

- Happiness is always available; it's *not* a reward for doing the "right" things.

Materials

- Cleansing tools of your choice

- A white candle

- A notebook or journal and a writing instrument such as a pen or pencil

Instructions

1. Begin by using a cleansing method of your choice, such as sound, smoke cleansing, or doing energy work. Affirm to yourself that you are open to a new, expansive way of life and ready to shuck off limitations.

2. Light your white candle and say the following out loud: "I light the way for guiding me, release these limits, and step up as free." Repeat this until it feels right. As you do this, take note of what comes up in your body and where you feel it (e.g., a release of tension in your shoulders).

3. In your notebook, write down what came up for you during the chant—where you felt it and the associated emotions or emotional progression that came with it.

4. Suspending judgment, explore the following questions in your notebook. This isn't another opportunity to feel bad about yourself—this is liberation!

   • What are some invisible cages you are aware of in your own world? Which ones feel particularly strong? Where did they come from, and how have they been reinforced?

   • Who is the most free and expansive version of you? How different are they from your current self?

   • Freewrite about an unlimited life. What would it look like? How would it pave the way for happiness?

Once you've completed this ritual, move through your life looking for opportunities to test out the waters (even in the smallest ways) of stepping up as your best unlimited self. It feels good to be free!

Become an Energetic Match for Joy

If you fuck with spiritual circles at all, chances are you're familiar with manifestation. Manifestation is a concept most famously linked to the Law of Attraction, although there are other "laws" that are similar in nature (the Law of Assumption, for example). Probably the most mainstream of the Universal Laws, the Law of Attraction is a collection of ideas, or "laws," about how the Universe operates, dating back to ancient cultures. It states that your mind has power over the creation of your reality, but more specifically that your "vibes" (a.k.a. the energies you carry and give off) have the power to attract that which you are seeking. As the often quoted saying goes, "You do not attract what you want, you attract what you *are*," and this *includes* what you believe to be true and available.

Whether or not you "believe" in manifesting, your thoughts, attitudes, and beliefs toward the world *are* influencing your lived experience. This is obvious on those days where you relentlessly fumble your way through with a bad attitude to match. However, it's also there on those special occasions where nothing can steal your joy. We as individuals can experience truly magical shifts when we learn to direct our *focus* and our *energy*, using our *intent* to create *magic from the mundane*.

Although manifestation in the mainstream is very focused on attracting tangible prosperity of some sort (more clients for your business, increased money flow, or other items), mystic-minded folks know that these principles are incredibly valuable when used to shift your emotional states and overall wellness. Witches accomplish this through shifting their personal energetics.

Everyone has a personal energy field that is influenced by their emotional states. This is that energy you can feel when you walk into a room where people have been fighting, or the passionate electricity that emerges between people who are about to kiss. While reading this, you can probably think of some examples of when you have felt this in action for yourself.

The concept of becoming an energetic match for what you are trying to call in is based on this idea of personal energetics. Imagine yourself as a radio, with the ability to tune in to different frequencies by shifting your personal energy. For example, if you are wanting to attract more joy into your life, you must become adept at feeling *into* joy. This means that you take the time to practice what joy feels like in your body and mind. This is the secret sauce to manifesting. You can write out goals all day long, but in becoming an energetic match for what you are trying to achieve, you call it in faster and align yourself more readily to being able to receive it.

Now, clearly this topic is much broader than one simple entry in this book could cover, but it's important to know this: If you are seeking happiness, feeling into the positives in your life will help you get there more quickly, regardless of your belief in energetics or manifesting. The only belief that is nonnegotiable to achieve this is that happiness is an *available* outcome for you. This is why you spent the first part of this book examining your core attitudes regarding what is possible. Happiness is always available within you to be summoned. This is clear when you close your eyes and conjure up some treasured memory of frolicking on the beach or lying in the embrace of a loved one, and you get the opportunity to relive those special moments and experience the accompanying emotions.

Embodiment of these emotions is the next step. Embodiment is the idea that you can become the physical representation or a channel for something intangible. Using the joy example, you can embody joy not only by feeling into it but by *truly living* in a joyful way—allowing the feeling to vibrate deep within your body and spirit. The magic of embodiment is that you can become such a clear channel that you influence others. Most people have met someone like this. In fact, very young children are a prime example of joyful embodiment. Many preschoolers (prior to picking up the limiting beliefs and programming that accumulate with growing up) are so adept at embodying joy that theirs becomes contagious.

So if you want to live a more joyful and happy life, take the time to sit with those feelings. When you call upon happy memories or conjure up the feeling of joy, notice *how* it feels and *where* it feels. If something like dancing to some ridiculous bop or going out and crunching leaves brings you joy, then get your witchy ass out and do that! Make room for it to be welcome. Bask in the feeling. Let it move through you and savor it for as long as possible. Seek opportunities to hack into your joy by doing the things or thinking the things that make you happy. Practice sitting with joy, contentment, and gratitude.

A Meditation for Matching Joy

Use this meditation to become an energetic match for joy.

1. Sit down comfortably in a safe place where you won't be disturbed.

2. Inhale through your nose (for approximately four counts), then exhale for approximately six counts.

3. Repeat for a total of six deep breaths, visualizing that you are inhaling joyful, positive energy and exhaling limitations, anxieties, and attachments to things that are weighing you down.

4. When you've done this cycle, continue mindfully breathing, but without the counts or visualizations, for ten more cycles (more is fine, too, but fewer would not be as effective).

5. State out loud: "I align my energy to the frequency of joy. I allow it to bloom within me and move through me, body and spirit."

6. Now think back to one of your most joyful happy memories. Try to recall it in such a way that you are essentially revisiting the experience. What sensations are present internally and externally? How do you feel? Try to sit with this feeling for as long as you can, truly savoring it. When it fades, allow yourself to feel gratitude for having had an experience that was so abundant with joy that you are able to reexperience it over and over through the portal of memory.

7. Lean into the feeling of gratitude as deeply as you can. Let this be proof that joy is possible and attainable, and that it can be conjured up using just your mind alone. Affirm to yourself that happiness is *always* within your grasp. Feel free to write in your journal how this went for you or if anything came up.

Banish the Bad and Treat Yourself to a Glow-Up

Witches are very adept at navigating liminal spaces, or the spaces *between* things. The space between the magic and the mundane. The space between the physical and spirit realms. The space between the light and the dark. However, there is another liminal space that you operate in that is less clear because you are so steeped in it: the space between who you are now and who you're eager to become.

Most of us have some idea of the person we want to become. It's not that you're not good enough as you are; it's just that having an idea of how you want to feel and respond to life is extremely helpful for actually getting there. Forming this working concept of where you want to be in the future and what you need to shift in order to get there is very valuable intel. Often, when you struggle to manifest the life you want, it's because you haven't made the internal shifts necessary to be able to create it and hold it.

When trying to manifest the future you want, you have to ask yourself, "Who would I need to be in order to receive this?" and "What are that future self's beliefs, goals, and attitudes?" For example, if a person believes that they are unlikely to live a life full of positive feelings, they likely struggle to find happiness because they don't see it as an *available* outcome. Even during happy or joyful moments, this person may have a hard time holding on to it if they carry the belief that struggle is the norm.

This isn't to say that you aren't good enough as you are and don't deserve happiness now; it's just that your belief systems might need a little decluttering. It's time to banish the bad shit and treat yourself to a glow-up!

For the witch especially, embracing this natural rhythm of shedding and regeneration on your own terms is immensely empowering. We all shift and evolve, whether we are consciously aware of it or not. When you approach this process in an intentional way, you empower yourself as the architect of your own life. Through taking the reins over your mindset, you can open up to the possibility that good things are always available to you and solidify your belief that you are worthy of them.

When dreaming about the things you want and who you want to be, ask yourself, "What needs to be dropped in order for me to hold this happiness?" Then, use the following scrub to let it go.

A Banishing and Rebirth Body Scrub

The following magical recipe is meant to help you scrub off all the energetic baggage that's holding you back, so you will be cleansed and renewed—able to rise up stronger and free of the BS!

Materials

- ½ cup coconut oil
- 6 drops lavender essential oil
- 6 drops lemon essential oil
- ½ cup finely ground sea salt*

*If your salt is too coarse, feel free to give it a few pulses in a food processor. The finer the better, so you don't harm your skin. Additionally, do not use a salt scrub on broken skin or wounds!

In a medium bowl, mix the coconut oil with the essential oils. Add the salt and mix until the desired consistency, adding more oil or salt if needed. Pour your mix into an airtight container, taking care not to let any water into the container. Provided no water gets into your jar, this scrub should keep for a few months (any moisture in the container will cause spoilage sooner).

In the shower, grab a generous scoop of your mixture using your fingers and gently scrub your body, imagining that it is scouring off all the baggage that is keeping you from moving into the next chapter of your happiness. Visualize all that limiting baggage going down the drain, leaving you refreshed, cleansed, and ready to step into a thriving version of yourself.

Hack Your Senses

Ever seen that meme that is a screenshot of an online questionnaire with the question "Are you a sentient human being?" and three answer options ("Yes," "No," and "Unfortunately"), the final option being chosen? Being a sentient human *does* feel unfortunate at times. This gift humans have, the ability to think and feel and conceptualize, is akin to a superpower when you think on it. However, living this reality can feel like a bloody curse sometimes!

The brain is an adept time traveler: It loves to play reruns of your biggest blunders and project your forecasted future upon the canvas of what's yet to be. What's a real challenge for this big ol' hunk of meat between your ears is living fully in the moment. Melting into the present and experiencing it fully with all of your sensory capabilities. Which is probably why using your senses is recommended in various therapies to ground and re-center yourself when your mind begins to spiral. A great example of this is the 5-4-3-2-1 grounding technique, where an individual overcome with racing thoughts and anxieties is tasked with naming five things they can see, four things they can feel, three things they can hear, two things they can smell, and one thing they can taste. The purpose of this exercise is to get a person grounded back into their body, rather than becoming quite untethered by an emotional thought spiral.

But what if you could use your brain's time-traveling capabilities, along with sensory experiences and a magical practice, to hack your mood? Everyone has those very specific sensory triggers that take them places without their consent. They transport you through time and space and hijack your emotions. The scent of your passed loved one's perfume can reduce you to tears, while the taste of your favorite meal can provide comfort. Somewhere along the line, your brain made a connection between a sensory experience and an emotional state, and this connection can act as a freeway to get to that place again, often regardless of other external factors.

Once you become aware of these sensory triggers, you can use them to your advantage. Not only will you know what to avoid if you want to feel a specific way, but you'll be able to use this knowledge to hack your body system, putting it into alignment with the emotions that you *do* want. If the scent of Bulgarian lavender makes you feel like a Zen, witchy queen, then why not use that info to your advantage to boost your craft? Your sensory experiences can act as a wormhole into a feeling, and you can utilize this to shift your frequency in a powerful way.

Continuing to use the example of scent, imagine a person who grew up baking with a grandparent and associated the scent of vanilla with happiness, comfort, and joy. Now, whenever this person catches a whiff of vanilla, they get a quick jolt of happiness and comfort in the chaos of adult life. In this example, the scent of vanilla is a key to unlocking a vibe—here the vibe is happiness. Although you aren't taught to exploit your own senses and manipulate your emotions like this, using the craft in this way can be immensely helpful for getting in (and out of) certain headspaces. This is the kind of mundane sorcery that I live for!

Scent is a prime example of this phenomenon, but it can happen with any sense. Maybe looking at sunflowers makes you feel joy, or maybe it's the color yellow or the sensation of sand between your toes. This is good shit to know! Whatever it is, I urge you to utilize this info to get you to the happy mindset you deserve to be in. This is a key component of witchcraft and how you will use it to hack your mood: using symbol, ritual, and self-knowledge in order to heal and transform.

Life and happiness are not a one-size-fits-all, so find out what fits *you* in this practice. This means asking yourself what your unique sensory codes are, good *and* bad. Write out a list, and pay keen attention as you move through life when you're triggered into one of these sensory-induced emotional states. Make note of it, and don't brush it off. It could help you out of a jam in the future and provide great information for your spellcraft and other witchy rituals!

A Recipe and Ritual to Hack Your Senses

This activity will guide you in how to "bottle a vibe," which you can use as you go forward in order to shift your moods and hack your sensory experience.

Materials

- Cleansing tools of your choice
- A small bowl
- Skin-safe carrier oil (grapeseed or olive; enough to fill roller bottle or vial)
- 6–12 drops essential oil(s) in your preferred scent(s)*

- A small roller bottle or vial (a 10-milliliter roller bottle is the standard)

*This scent(s) should be something you associate with joy and happiness!

Instructions

1. Cleanse yourself, your space, and your materials however you choose.

2. In a bowl, mix your carrier oil with your essential oil(s) until well blended.

3. Carefully pour your mix into your small bottle or vial and label it.

4. Take your oil and anoint your body, placing a small amount or drop of oil on each of your wrists, your collarbone, the center of your rib cage, the small of your back, and the soles of your feet.

5. Now take slow, deep breaths, allowing the scent to wash over and through you. Pay attention to the feelings that come up and try to "anchor" them in your body with mindful awareness. To call in the frequency of joy, you can also pair this ritual with a song that uplifts you and/or magical movement—whatever helps you embody joy and happiness. Enjoy this task; there is no way to do this wrong! It is simply an opportunity to move with and call in a feeling.

6. Write out your experiences after this ritual in your book of shadows, if it's helpful.

Learn When to Quit

"Quitters never win!" Odds are good that you've heard this statement, or some variation of it, before. Our culture holds perseverance and "pushing through" in high regard, which makes sense for the most part, especially in the context of capitalism. And, of course, the ability to keep on keepin' on in challenging situations is a virtue. But the shadow side to this is that you likely don't give quitting (or giving up) the credit that it's due as an equally empowered action toward shaping the life you want. There is big magic in quitting, pausing, and reevaluating your goals and your attitudes as you move through life. Sometimes thriving isn't just about what you want to call in or prioritize; it's about learning when to say *enough* and shifting gears. As witches know, life is full of opposing forces that are equally valid and relevant. So it is no surprise that magic is the same. You must call in and release, summon and banish. Halting or quitting something in order to make space for better is just part of the process—an incredibly valuable part, when you're aiming to seek happiness.

In your efforts to seek happiness, you embark on various roads, like The Fool of the tarot, gleefully stepping off the cliff into the cheerful unknown! New relationships, pursuing educational or career opportunities, and creating goals for yourself that you think will bring you joy are just a few examples of these roads. Although some of these lead to favorable outcomes, others simply lead you to see the things you *don't* want. Sometimes you unknowingly tether yourself to dreams you've outgrown. This can result in achieving big things and realizing that you don't want them anymore. Obviously, you can be left feeling some type of way about this!

You are in a constant state of flux. Who you are and what you desire shifts and changes as you move through life. What made you happy at one point might not necessarily at another. What your values are may even shift with time and experience. For this reason, it is important that you be open to reevaluating what you want on an ongoing basis. As you grow and evolve, so should your goals, desires, expectations, and attitudes toward the world.

Can you think of a time that you worked toward something you *thought* would make you happy, only to find yourself frustrated or even overwhelmed by the process? This is common and can pop up often in the context of personal development work. And if it's something that you truly want, it can be incredibly empowering to just put that shit on pause. There is no emotional, logical, or energetic value to banging your head against the wall in vain. In many cases you may be tempted to abandon these things in your frustration, but it can help to simply give yourself permission to put it on ice. You can decide your next steps later.

In a world that glamorizes busyness and constant motion, it can be incredibly empowering to take back the reins and declutter your desires, choosing happiness by being discerning about what you're giving your energy to. Saying "no" (or at least "not right now") is an incredibly important aspect of curating your life. Imagine a bookcase that is full: Half the books are kind of bad or no longer interest you, and half of them are good and you may want to reread them later. Since the shelf is full, if you want more good books, you will have to clear out some of the books you don't need or want any more to make space for them. The same goes for your life: Sometimes you gotta clear out the old to make way for the new!

A Spell to Pause and Regroup

The following spell will help you take a break or energetic pause for perspective from the things you may have been chasing out of habit rather than intention.

Materials

- Cleansing tools of your choice

- Paper and a pen

- Ice cube tray

- Moon water*

*To make moon water, place some filtered water in a clear Mason jar with a lid under the light of the full moon overnight.

Instructions

1. Do your chosen cleansing rituals and open your magical space.

2. Pick something that you need to take a good break from. Not something you necessarily want to banish completely—this is more about getting a wee perspective break.

3. Write it down on a small strip of paper and roll it up.

4. Place the paper in the ice cube tray and pour the moon water over it, stating aloud your intention to halt this thing for your best good. Thank yourself for having the wisdom to halt this thing in the interest of your best good.

5. Place in the freezer for as long as you want the break to be. You may want to set a calendar reminder so that you do not forget your spell and have unintended shifts in motivation toward the thing you're pausing.

6. When you are ready to get back to it, take your cube and place it out by the side of your home to melt and be reabsorbed into the earth.

Shift Your Focus

In a constantly connected society, it becomes clear that our attention is our currency. How are you spending yours?

We exist in a time where you can find out what's happening pretty much anywhere in the world with just a few taps of a finger. Our awareness is inundated with screens—TVs, smartphones, tablets, and computers. There was a time when we had to wait until the next newspaper or airing of the news on TV to get information. Now we can watch the world in real time. Isn't it magical! Not only do you have to think about the madness in your own circles, but it feels like you also have to concern yourself about every single thing occurring on a global scale. Energetically, it's draining and emotionally consuming.

This occurs because digital media hijacks our awareness. Human beings are emotional creatures: We have immense capacity for empathy. While this served well in an evolutionary sense in the past, within the current context it can feel as if you're constantly getting emotionally jerked around by the chaos that is pushed straight into the palms of your hands. This acts as a hole in your energetic bucket, causing you to feel depleted and strained. Good-intentioned empathy is played on for clicks, benefiting nobody but advertisers and media companies.

A key foundation of a happy life is to cultivate your awareness. When you realize the power of your thoughts over your perception of reality (a power most witches use to their advantage), paying keen attention to where your focus goes becomes a no-brainer. Viewing your attention as your currency just makes sense when you know just how valuable it is. Most people are caught up in habits that spend their attention in all the wrong ways, and they lose precious peace for it. It's draining in both a magical and mundane sense. This isn't to say that you shouldn't be informed or that you shouldn't care about injustices and things that are happening out there. You *absolutely* should. You just need to have boundaries and figure out where your actions will have the best impact...and honey, disaster-scrolling ain't it!

Here's the thing: The more you can do to shift your focus back to your immediate sphere, the better. It's a noble thing to care and want to heal the world, but the reality is that you can achieve this better by calling your wandering energy back into nourishing your own self and life. There is no benefit to having your energy be siphoned off by things you have little control over when there are surely things in your own sphere that could use tending to. Things that you *do* have power over. By shifting your focus toward your own well-being, you heal yourself. And as you heal yourself, you heal those around you through the energy you bring to the world and your relationships. If you are truly wanting to make a difference from afar, there are many high-impact ways to do so (donations, raising awareness, or educating yourselves and others) while still keeping your energetic boundaries and not flooding your awareness with drama just for the sake of being connected.

And this goes beyond just news. When you fixate too long on the things you *don't* have or the ways you feel you don't measure up, these imagined shortcomings keep you in a state of lack and perceived inferiority. Understandably, it can be very challenging to feel content in these conditions. This can be a sneaky blind spot for personal development seekers and spiritual practitioners if they aren't careful. Awareness of a problem is the first step to finding a solution, sure, but what happens sometimes is that you focus so much on "fixing" the problem that the problem itself is held in the center of your awareness, where it is more keenly felt. And I'm not saying that toxic positivity or emotional bypassing is the solution. The solution is to know yourself and trust yourself enough to throw yourself a pity party, but give yourself a curfew!

What you choose to linger your gaze upon and the beliefs you hold to be true work together to paint your reality. All the ingredients for emotional states such as happiness exist within you and can be teased out by environmental cues. By cultivating your awareness and decluttering your belief systems, you are more easily able to shift your emotional states in ways that actually serve you. Transformation is the wheelhouse of the witch. They know that joy can be found in the darkest corners and that the bad sads don't need to linger forever. But most importantly, they can clearly see just how much power they can assert over their experience of life, simply by making adjustments to where they put their focus.

A Candle and Commitment Ritual to Shift Your Focus

This can help you shift your focus back to where it will be of better benefit for your life and your wellness.

Materials

- Cleansing tools of your choice
- A small bowl
- Salt (enough to fill small bowl)
- A white candle
- A sharp object like a thumbtack
- 2 clear quartz stones

Instructions

1. Begin by cleansing yourself and your space and casting any protection you prefer. This ritual is best done in a safe, quiet space where you are unlikely to be disturbed.

2. Fill the small bowl with salt.

3. Take your white candle and carve these words into it: "Energy come back to me." Hold your candle between your palms and set the intention that this will be a beacon, calling your energy back into where it can serve you better.

4. Close your eyes and ask that upon opening them, your awareness will be cleansed and focused back on your own joy and healing.

5. Place your candle in the bowl of salt and light it.

6. Sit before your candle with 1 clear quartz crystal in each hand. Begin deep breathing, deliberately inhaling through your nose and exhaling through your mouth to get into a meditative state.

7. While still holding your crystals, open your arms up as if you were going for a big hug (you can remain seated or stand up for this).

8. In your head or out loud, state the intention to call all your wandering energy back into yourself. Visualize it flowing in toward your chest, filling you up, and leaving you feeling invigorated and refreshed.

Celebrate Consciousness

The human brain is an incredible piece of machinery; however, as most brain-owners can testify, it can also be a huge pain in the ass. It has a natural tendency to fixate on the negative while dismissing the positive. That being said, you are also wholly capable of retraining your thoughts in a more positive direction, whether you identify as a witch or not. This isn't to say you should repress or bypass your negative emotions; you can simply make efforts to give the positive ones like gratitude some more balanced airtime!

Gratitude is one of those positive emotions that's crucial for unlocking joy, and it's not really surprising when you look at it from a mindset perspective. Considering that your mindset and what you choose to focus on play such a key role in your experience of life, it just makes sense that taking inventory of the good things would be beneficial to your well-being. Mainstream science backs this up as well. There have been many studies done on gratitude, and results have indicated that focusing on gratitude can make you happier and healthier and improve your relationships, work performance, and outlook on life. All fantastic shifts for a happier life!

That being said, for many, gratitude can be challenging and bring up all sorts of feels. There are points in life where you can feel so stuck and lost that finding the ability to see the good things feels borderline impossible. One of my favorite things to cling to in these moments is gratitude for consciousness itself: Although the ability to think and feel can be gut-wrenching at times, it *is* a gift. You are so powerful by way of the mind—to create, to feel, and to understand things. These are the cornerstones of the human experience. There is big magic in the simple fact that you are a sentient being, able to experience this chaotic whirlwind of life. This is the kind of gift witches celebrate as they channel their feelings into a spell and tap in to their senses during a vibey ritual.

Recently, I had a big blowup with someone close to me. I stormed out the door and pulled out my phone with the intention of listening to something about as ragey as I felt, but instead I noticed my husband's shower-time playlist. This list is nothing but ridiculously feel-good, guilty pleasure–type tunes. And although that was the last thing I *felt* like listening to, I knew that doing so would be the best thing for my simmering rage. Begrudgingly, I turned it on, and the first song was "Separate Ways (Worlds Apart)" by Journey. Now, this song is a synthesizer cheese-fest of epic proportions—the exact kind of song meant for an angsty 1980s movie conflict montage...which made me realize the absurdity of the situation I was in. Here I was, thirty-eight years old and angrily stomping around like a disgruntled teenager with the soundtrack to match. I started laughing uncontrollably, and the feeling of joy washed over me. I found the situation so absurdly hilarious and was overwhelmed with gratitude and amazement that I could shift through very intense emotional states all within the confines of my own skull.

This is the magic of consciousness. Just the simple ability to be able to see and experience even your hardest struggles is such an unsung treasure. It's what moves you, what lights a fire under you, and what gives color to your existence. Even in the hardest of times, comfort can be found in simply feeling grateful for your emotional and intellectual faculties. Retrain your brain to see the good and be grateful for it. Celebrate the simple fact that you are capable of the awareness to see and experience even your struggles.

Affirmations to Celebrate Consciousness

Personally, I love doing affirmations out loud in front of a mirror. It feels like I am giving myself loving permission, and I feel more connected to the messages. This is likely because not only am I creating them, I am saying them out loud, watching myself say them, and hearing them! The following are just some ideas to get you started; however, it can be really powerful to create your own affirmations. The only guideline is that you make these affirming statements in a declarative way ("I am," "I will," etc.).

- My consciousness is an asset, even when it might not feel like it.

- I am capable of making big emotional shifts without needing something external to push me.

- I commit to honoring my felt experience and not placing judgments upon it.

- I am grateful for the faculties of my brain, even when it's being a troublesome bitch.

- I have the power to radically shift my mindset and challenge belief systems that do not serve me.

- I am grateful for big feelings and the uncomfortable ways that they move me.

- I am grateful for my intelligence and the ability to spot problems and seek to solve them.

- As an empowered witch, I am able to shift my mindset to open the doors of possibility.

- I am grateful for the pleasures and pains of this human experience and how they help me evolve.

- I have the power to shift my awareness to the positive, even when doing so is a challenge. I am up for the task.

Keep It Risky

Up until my thirties, I took great pride in my calculated approach to living. I wore my cautious nature like a badge of honor, spending a lot of time envisioning the worst-case scenario, and ultimately came to the conclusion that unless I was willing to accept that as my fate, any moves should be avoided. Does this sound familiar?

Although there is nothing wrong with being cautious, an approach to life like this is based too much on control. Sure, you can't mess up if you never make a move. However, this safety comes at a cost. At the end of the day, you are still powerless over many things, and the desire to control things is, in turn, reinforced by this behavior. You can become so wrapped up in limiting beliefs about the world that you miss out on much of the fun and adventure it has to offer.

Great things are simply not as available to those who fear leaving their carefully structured safe places. You have to meet struggles with control head-on and dismantle them in order to pave the way for opportunity and to truly thrive. Remember: The self-empowered witch understands that seeking happiness isn't just a process of magically calling in; it's also a process of magical *release*.

Now, obviously an aversion to risks can be wise and adaptive. I'm not advocating missing your rent due date to jump out of an airplane or eating that sketchy thing your toddler just handed you. What I *am* saying is that in the chaos of the uncertain, yes, there is potential for destruction, but there is also the potential for a joyful, abundant life that you may never have considered possible. It's important to be discerning and to connect with your inner guidance. Pushing through fear can be a doorway to tremendous happiness—a gift that you can bestow upon yourself.

As a magically empowered witch, never underestimate the power of choosing expansion, challenging yourself, and being open to explore the riskier path, even if you ultimately decide not to take it. Reframe any limiting beliefs you may be holding on to when it comes to taking risks or choosing a path less traveled. Risk doesn't have to be all doom and gloom or a gamble that's guaranteed to go wrong. In many circumstances, it can be the secret sauce for a happier life.

A Comfort in Risk Spell Jar

The following spell will help you feel safe and magically supported, even while taking on risks and tackling new things.

Materials*

- Cleansing tools of your choice
- A small jar
- Himalayan pink salt
- Dried rosemary
- Dried lavender buds
- Dried yarrow
- An orange chime candle

*The amount you will need for each ingredient will depend on the size of your jar. You will be layering these in equal amounts; about 1 teaspoon of each should suffice for a small jar.

Instructions

1. Begin by cleansing yourself, your space, and your materials using whichever method you choose.

2. In your jar, begin layering your ingredients in the following order: salt, rosemary, lavender, yarrow. The salt and rosemary act as a protective foundation, the lavender is for comfort and calm in the face of chaos, and the yarrow on top is for strength and healing.

3. Light your orange candle and reflect on the role of chaos and uncertainty in the natural world. Even in the most balanced of ecosystems, there are random events and a great deal of uncertainty. Nature itself is chaotic and wild, despite humankinds's efforts to understand and decode it.

4. Affirm to yourself that risk is not always a bad thing, and that amazing things lie on the other side of fear. Lean into the terrifying thrill of letting go of control!

5. Put a lid on your jar, then take your candle and drip the wax over the lid to seal it.

6. Whenever you feel like you could use a boost of this fear-busting magic, shake up the jar.

Awaken to Your Power

Modern life can feel all sorts of icky at times, and the constant availability of information makes the injustices and BS in the world feel that much more in-your-face. It's a situation where a lot of humanity feels disempowered on a collective scale, on top of the disempowerment people can feel on an individual level, where you may see yourself as just a cog in the machine, getting jerked around by your job, your family, society, and whatever else happens to pop up.

But, although there are certainly things you have no power over, you have a lot more power than you probably give yourself credit for. Are there things that make you unhappy that you have no control over? Of course. Any other answer would be bypassing the very real struggles you face in life. That being said, working on shifting your mindset to a more empowered place is an incredible tool you have at your disposal. And even more lucky for you, witches are masters of harnessing this skill.

Back in the 1960s, a psychologist named Julian Rotter explored the concept of "locus of control." This is the degree to which people feel power over their lives and what happens to them. It is a spectrum, with an internal locus of control on one end and an external locus of control on the other. Where someone falls on this scale is uniquely personal and shapes their motivations and attitudes toward life. Those who have a high internal locus of control are more likely to believe that they have power over their lives, whereas those with a high external locus of control typically believe that life is being inflicted upon them.

For example, if a person with a high internal locus of control gets passed over for a promotion, they're likely to take responsibility for this, thinking that they weren't performing up to speed and that this is something they can work on. On the other hand, a person with a high external locus of control might believe they were passed over because their boss just doesn't like them or because of some other outside issue they have no control over. Alternatively, should the people in this example get the promotion, the person with an internal locus of control would likely feel they accomplished this based on their performance, whereas the person with an external locus of control might think it was a fluke.

This illustrates the profound importance of *feeling* empowered. When you feel as if your actions and behaviors make a difference, you align yourself as an active agent in your own life and well-being. This is *your* life, and *you* are the main character in it. Your actions matter, and your happiness is important. Witches know that we hold the keys to shift our own experience of life, in our happiness and our healing.

In your darkest moments, it can feel not only as if you are helpless, but as if you may not matter at all. But here's the thing: Your existence has rippled through the world in ways you may not be aware of. At some point your smile or kind words may have shifted someone's day, which may have shifted their life or the lives they encountered. No one is an island, and you matter in ways that may not be immediately apparent. Even if you feel like you've done nothing at all for this to be the case, it is still true. You don't have to *do* anything in order to make an impact; it just happens regardless.

So although it can feel as if you have no power in this modern world, it's important to know that you are a magical, empowered being as your birthright. There is so much joy to be had in this! As a witch, you have the power to heal and transform. You are powerful. Awaken to this magic!

A Visualization and Movement Practice to Awaken Your Power

This activity can be used to lean into the feelings of empowerment and fluid, ecstatic joy that come with awakening to your power.

1. Find a safe, quiet space where you are unlikely to be disturbed. Put on some calm but powerful music (something without lyrics is best), and use whatever method you like to cleanse and protect your space.

2. Sit and begin deep breathing (in through the nose and out through the mouth) to ground and center yourself. As you breathe, with each inhale, imagine that your body is being filled with powerful and strong energy. Imagine this energy you're receiving as filling you up so much that it overflows, creating a powerful aura that surrounds you. This is your energetic body: expansive and charged. With each exhale, visualize yourself releasing all the traumas and negativity that have accumulated through your life.

3. Now rise up if you are able, still visualizing this energy flowing in and around you. Begin to move in whichever way feels right for you based on the music, your mood, or whatever else. Follow your instincts—humans are made for this!

4. As you move, conceptualize yourself as a powerful, sovereign being. This is *always* the case, underneath all the drama. In this moment it is just you, stripped from society, stripped from the limitations of thought, stripped down to just a spirit with a body. Allow yourself to feel totally and completely free and untethered. Nobody is watching, so move with joy. Literally dance like nobody's watching!

5. As you continue to dance, think of the many miracles that had to occur in order for you to exist. Think of the lives you've touched, perhaps when you weren't even aware of it. Think of the immense power you have over your own life and your own destiny. Let these thoughts fill you with expansive joy and the feeling of empowerment. You are so much more than just a body or a cog in the machine. You are a powerful being, a miracle in the flesh, and a spirit that was meant to soak up all the joy that life has to offer. Feel it.

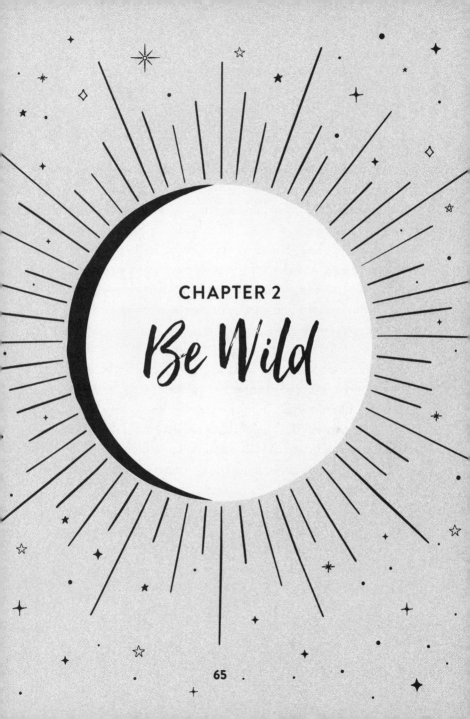

CHAPTER 2

Be Wild

As children, we are often encouraged to spend our days exploring the outdoors and relentlessly pursuing joy in it. However, in adulthood we find ourselves separated more and more from the earth—and from the happiness it offers. We replace playing outside with working in front of a screen, then mindlessly scrolling through another screen. Here's the thing, though: As animals of the wild, we are *meant* to be part of nature, not to be insulating ourselves from it and fighting to keep it out. While I'm not advocating to sell all your stuff to go live in a cave, what I *am* saying is that we have created a very high hill of disconnection in the modern age, and that by grounding ourselves in our animal nature and welcoming more wild into our lives we celebrate our place in this system and can unlock even more dimensions of living joyfully free!

Witches understand the deep and purposeful value of nourishing this connection with nature, and recognize that in doing so, we nourish our connection to self and to spirit. Much of spellcraft utilizes earth's medicines, and many witchcraft rituals involve honoring the healer that's underfoot. In this chapter, you will use the inherently wild elements of magic to find joy and ease, including worshipping the ground and getting outside and reclaiming your natural instincts.

Gaze at the Sky in Wonder

Our ancestors, delightfully Internet-free, used to look to the sky for entertainment and guidance. Weather could be predicted through interpreting the clouds, and navigation was made possible through charting the movement of celestial objects. They watched the birds fly and the storms roll in, and made inferences from that. Spiritually, the sky played an integral role in many great myths and legends; it was the backdrop of both creation and cautionary tales. Creatively, the sky played (and still plays) muse to musicians and poets who speak of staring up at the same stars as the people they love. In the human heart, the sky has a very unique place. It is a mysterious realm that is simultaneously constant and wildly unpredictable.

As human life evolved, so too did the methods of info dissemination. Now we can curl up in front of a screen to check the weather, and it can be all too easy to be so involved with what is happening in the mundane human realms that we can fail to look up at the magic that exists above us. How much has our species lost touch with by disrupting the place of human observation in interpreting the world?

Here's the thing: You are *of* nature. You were born from it. And while modern progress is a thing of wonder, it has also left a void when it comes to natural alignment. There is something so simple and beautiful about being able to interpret the sky, to allow yourself the slow pleasure of being entertained by the movement of clouds or the dazzling thrill of a meteor shower! Some definitions of happiness are keen to point out the particular satisfaction that comes about with living with purpose. The dissolution of your relationship with nature for interpreting and predicting the natural cycles of which you are a part is a divergence from purpose, and you might be missing out on the unique interconnected joy that comes with this.

Reclaim this magic!

Witches are usually a little ahead of the game when it comes to looking skyward. Many witches incorporate celestial cycles into their practice, typically by using astrology or tracking moon phases. They aim to live in deep alignment with these natural processes like their ancestors long ago. As those who practice will tell you, going out to speak to the moon and to gaze at the sunrise are valid spells. It's humbling to stare at the sky and feel the weight of your problems become dwarfed by the wonders of nature. It's a small and meaningful rebellion against a tide that would keep sweeping you away from your divine nature.

So if you're looking for a way to reclaim that spark of connection you've lost in the advancements and hustle of modern life, try looking up. Observe the clouds, the moon, and the stars. You are surrounded by so much beauty. Train yourself to see the sky, to bask in the seeing, and to appreciate the joy and wonder that can come from living under such a beautiful, wonderous thing.

A Skygazing Practice

This is a simple routine to help you connect with the sky and the intentional joy and wonder that can come from mindfully appreciating its presence in your life.

Materials

- A notebook or journal and a writing instrument such as a pen or pencil
- 2 weeks to commit to this practice

Week 1

1. Get up and spend a few minutes outside every morning. Observe the sky and write or draw what you see. Are there clouds? What do they look like? What colors do you see? Are they in motion?

2. As you observe the sky, breathe mindfully. Consider the relationship your ancestors would have had with the sky before the age of modern distractions.

3. As you move through your day, try to remember to gaze up at the sky a few times and take 3–6 deep breaths in through your nose and out through your mouth. Take note of how you feel. Is this helpful for you to gain perspective or realign yourself?

Week 2

1. Take a few minutes every evening to gaze at the sky. Can you see stars? The moon? Do you know the locations of any planets or constellations? Are you interested in learning?

2. Breathe deeply and meditate on how human problems shrink when you are faced with the vastness of the cosmos.

3. Write down your thoughts or mood after doing this. You can also try to draw what you see if you wish.

Bonus Activity: Learn about different cloud formations and what they indicate weather-wise so that you can begin to learn to interpret the weather on your own.

Have Yourself a Frolic

If there is one thing adulthood can teach us, it's the importance of play. I can declare with absolute certainty that the years I spent as a child were far superior to all this adulting garbage. Remember heading outside for what felt like an eternity on a summer's day, running and playing, zero fucks given to any grown-up nonsense?

The importance of play becomes abundantly clear in adulthood when the lack of it is keenly felt across the board. At no point in the life span is there a clear "cutoff" for play; however, somewhere along the line we trade in the abundant carefree joy of childhood for a more rigid and structured life experience. As we get older, the idea of what's "acceptable play" shifts from the aimless "joy just for the sake of it" kind of play into the realm of skill-building or competition. Hobbies, sports, and video games can be socially accepted forms of play for adults; however, it's much like creativity in the sense that you don't place much importance on engaging in play for the sake of the act itself. It's commonly acknowledged that a child's "job" is play: This is how they learn and grow as people. So why do people drift away from this as being a priority when it's so sorely needed in adulthood... when you could use its benefits the most?

The healing benefits of play are well documented and can be felt across the life span. Play can be relaxing and stress-relieving and can thrust you into the frequency of joy. A variety of activities and behaviors could be categorized as play; however, for the purpose here, you want to look at unstructured, unplugged play, preferably in nature. What you could use is a proper frolic! You should be kicking off your shoes, running with the breeze, and stuffing your pockets with pebbles like the unhinged, wild witch you are!

To honor your natural impulses and allow yourself the space to play just for the joy of it is to open a door to flow and alignment. This is mindful living magic in action: the simple act of *be*-ing in the moment, playing and having fun just for the sake of it. Not for results, not for bragging rights, but just to sink into the simple pleasure of *play for play's sake*. This is far beyond simply calling in joy; it is a reconnection to your animal nature. This is part of the allure of the witch's path. A witch knows the importance of honoring their wild as a connection to the divine. A witch knows that life is meant to be lived deliciously!

Adulthood doesn't have to be this boring landscape that's completely devoid of play. Chances are it's just the medicine you need when you're feeling tapped out and tired AF. So if you want to shift your mood and shimmy up to joy, get outside for a frolic!

A Nature Mandala

While it may feel tempting to do this out in nature, there are people out there who retreat to the woods in order to forget that people exist, so I personally try to do rituals like this in either public spaces like parks or private spaces like yards out of respect.

Materials

- A variety of natural items in multiples—for example, leaves, pine cones, sticks, flowers, etc. (these should be naturally fallen; please do not mess with nature just minding her own business)
- A small stone or pebble

Instructions

1. Begin by putting your hands on the ground and deep breathing as if you're doing a grounding exercise (because you are!). This is to help you get connected to the earth and to open the space for play.

2. Place your nature items in organized piles.

3. Put the stone or pebble on the ground, in the center of where your mandala will be, and set the intention to enjoy this time of idle play in nature. Then start arranging your other items around the stone or pebble in a circular pattern.

4. Keep adding more items in a pattern that continues to layer outward in a circular formation. Have fun with this and be creative!

5. When the mandala is complete, you can either leave it or disassemble it. Whatever feels good. The important thing is to do this activity with the kind of aimless joy that is typically not reserved for adulthood.

Let Nature Seduce You

Have you ever noticed how you can almost black out completely on that commute to work every day? It can be striking just how monotonous the days can feel in adulthood, many of them blending into this boring purgatory soup, when there is a whole juicy life to be lived if you just take the time to notice it!

Mindful awareness is one element of witchcraft (and many ancient and modern practices) that can disrupt this experience of living on autopilot. Mindfulness is being fully present and aware in the moment. When you take a beat to just breathe and be aware of all the things around you, you get sucked out of that weird limbo most people spend their days in, where they're thinking of the past or getting hung up on the future. There's good reason this concept endured from the Buddhist traditions of long ago all the way up to modern psychology and magical practice. This shit works, and it can radically transform your wellness.

Your senses are the key to getting to a grounded and mindful place. By tapping in to them, you can get sucked back into your body to experience the moment. And nature, with all of its wild sensory glory, is the perfect setting for trying to connect with the moment. In nature there are so many delicious sensations all around; to simply sit with your toes in the sand or lie in the grass is to experience a very simple and dramatically underrated magical experience. It can shift your mood, it can plant you right into this very moment, it can stir a very old remembering—ancestral memories deep within in your DNA that know the big power in this simple pleasure.

Many people get these primal urges to just kick off their shoes and play in the grass, or to be naked under the stars, but all too often they don't indulge. This strips them of prime opportunities for some much-needed joy. Allow nature to seduce you! When her grass whispers for your toes to come and play, listen. When she asks for you to smell the flowers, stop and inhale like it's your job! Adult life can become entirely too devoid of spontaneity and pleasure, and by nurturing this connection you honor the spark of wild divinity in you. This is what any witch longs for!

So go be naked in the sun! Run across a field in your bare feet! Lie out under the full moon! Get out of your head and back into the moment as quickly as you can to fully enjoy the experience of your one incredible life. It is your birthright to experience all the glory of this life. Whenever you can, allow yourself to come alive again in nature's arms. Ignore the inner voice that would have you sleeping on your own magic, and chase joy by making your interactions in the natural world a mindful and intentional sensory experience.

A Ritual to Mindfully Connect with Nature

Although mindful awareness can be practiced everywhere, doing so in nature supercharges the experience. To truly get an extra thrill from this, do it somewhere private where you can be fully naked to get the whole sensory experience.

1. Lie down on the ground in a safe place and close your eyes.

2. Begin deep breathing in through your nose and out through your mouth. As you inhale, feel yourself pulling in the calming, cleansing energy of the earth beneath you. As you exhale, imagine yourself expelling all the hectic energy of the modern world.

3. Continue breathing deeply, having an awareness of the ground underneath you—how it feels on your skin, the texture, the temperature. As you turn your attention toward the physical sensation of lying on the ground, follow your awareness to any other senses that are triggered by the environment. Any sounds, smells, physical sensations. Simply take note of them and where they pop up for you in your body, enjoy it, then move on.

4. Practice this mindfulness for as long as you're able to; there is no room for judgments with something like this! Allow yourself to lean into the feeling of gratitude toward the earth and toward yourself for practicing this skill!

5. Take note of your mood and overall well-being afterward, and whether this brought some happiness for you.

Create with Nature

Although I talk a lot of trash about the bizarre circumstances of contemporary human life, the fact is we have so much ease when it comes to basic survival. For instance, gathering food in the modern era is a lot less fraught with danger than it once was. Your chances of getting mauled by a bear on your morning coffee run, while not zero, are pretty small! There are obvious perks. Unfortunately, our spirits are left longing for something a little bit more when it comes to living with purpose.

In 2020, the world caught a really neat glimpse into the inner workings of the modern human spirit when many folks were told to stay home and turned to gardening, canning, bread-making, and more to ease the anxiety of a global pandemic. There was a nostalgic shift toward the old-fashioned way of life. It's really only in the last few generations that society has lost so much knowledge of and connection with the land in a survival sense, leaving that void you may feel now when it comes to purpose. Many witches aim to seek that purpose again through a meaningful relationship with nature.

There is a special pride to be taken in living in a connected and self-sufficient way. Does this mean that you should quit your job and turn to woodcutting and milling your own flour? Not necessarily. But in teaching yourself some basic skills to live in a way that is more connected to the larger natural world, you not only help yourself in a practical way but also open the doors to a deep sense of fulfillment that many have lost touch with. And this doesn't always need to be simply an exercise in survival.

Connecting with nature also helps you connect to a very meaningful source of purposeful joy.

Witchcraft is a practice where you can intentionally choose to engage in actions that help you strengthen your connection to the land, yourself, and the cosmos. You can use magic to tap in to the wild joy of living in tandem with nature as both caretaker and fawning acolyte. Beyond that, you can reclaim the very base human fulfilment that comes with doing tangible things that matter, whether it be through play or through necessity. So grow a garden, gather herb bundles for spellcraft, practice self-sufficiency in some way, or make rattles with seeds for some playful music or as a creative addition to witchy rituals. Do something purposeful in tandem with nature and see how it feels.

A Wildcraft Activity

Fun fact: Many overlooked weeds in most areas are actually edible, provided they are found under safe conditions (for instance, away from vehicle exhaust or sprayed chemicals). For example, in my own backyard there are usable weeds such as sweet violet, plantain, and yarrow. In the parks in the interior of British Columbia, you can ethically wildcraft* St. John's wort, juniper, and wild mint. My first book recommendation for novice witches is to grab a copy of a local plant guide (or guides!) for your area.

Next step: Go wandering! If you take up the habit of looking down and learning which plants are available, you might be surprised to find that you have a whole variety of usable plants for witchy (spells, etc.) or medicinal purposes. It really doesn't take a lot of time or effort to learn one plant at a time, watching its development through its life cycle and checking against various sources to ensure you are identifying the right one. Never ingest a plant if you are not 100 percent sure what it is! Local groups can be a good source of info from more experienced guides and foragers. There are folks out there meeting randos every day on dating apps, so why not shuck the romantic expectations and get to know a fellow plant weirdo?

By forging a connection with the local lands, you gain a deep connection with nature, which can give your spells some extra oomph when using your own grown or wildcrafted herbs. There is something very special and full circle about being able to pick some mint on a nice hike, then take it home to use for a tea ritual.

*Any witch planning to forage or wildcraft must first become familiar with ethical gathering practices, as these can vary by region and species!

Make a Date with the Wild

Every calendar day, we get up and move through life—but how often do we allow truly living to grace our calendar?

The old adage is true: You only have one life. Although you've likely heard this and have a solid understanding of what it means, putting the lesson it gives into practice feels a little more tricky. The reality is that the human experience is riddled with all sorts of priorities that don't make space for slow, intentional living or indulging your impulses. Well, I'm going to let you in on a little secret here: A happy life is one that's deliciously lived. Sink your teeth into your daily experience and allow it to drip down your chin! This is the essence of joy in action—being mindfully present in the brilliance of the everyday.

As part of living deliciously, you need to incorporate living—*truly living*—into your life. This will look different for every person. Some find long, leisurely walks on the beach to be *truly living*, while others hop outta planes. It's all relative! However, one way you can embrace living life to the fullest is to make space to do so as part of your ongoing routine. You live on a beautiful planet that's floating through space. You are illuminated and warmed by the sun, and you are watched and guided by the moon. You are a part of the mysterious cosmos and only here for a limited time. It would be a shame to let it go to waste!

So wake up early to watch the sunset, stay up until ridiculous hours to wish on shooting stars, take day trips to the beach for no other reason than to soak up its glory. Make dates with nature and commit to fully experiencing as much of the beauty and mystery as you can. After all, if boring stuff like going to the post office can take up space in your day, why can't chasing joy and sinking into experience? Each day in this big wide world is ripe with new experiences that you can enjoy if you make space for doing just that. Prioritize these "dates" and shower them with love and appreciation. What a gift it is to have this life that gives you multiple opportunities to sit with these often-overlooked miracles!

At the end of the day, feeling fatigued and overworn is a symptom of the modern human experience. So what's the difference if you lose a bit of sleep to watch an eclipse or a sunrise? If doing so will fill your cup with joy and leave you feeling more present and connected, take the time to pencil that in! How many sunrises are missed while mindlessly scrolling through phones in bed? How many fields are left unfrolicked in order to get to events that no one even wants to attend? In the daily monotony of endless routine, it is the responsibility to personal joy to create space to feel. To be aligned.

Life *can* be a struggle—that much is true. However, it is also a gift, for those who have eyes to see it. Let being alive romance you. Take comfort in the big, wide arms of Mother Earth. Like people, like art, like love, the magic in nature—in life—is often in the quirks and in the glory of experiencing it. Make time to do *that*.

An Enchanted Date

On a Friday (the day associated with Venus), write down one idea for a date you can make with your life in the upcoming week. This could be going to a river, watching a sunset, or anything else that is connected with the natural world. The idea is to take some time in an intentional way to just be present for an experience that is independent of other people, responsibilities, and the trappings of regular modern human life. Remind yourself that it can be as short and sweet as ten minutes. As you set off on your date, make sure you are framing it properly in your mind as being a positive addition and not a stressor. For example, if you are wanting to get up to watch the sunrise, allow yourself to be happy for the upcoming experience and not get caught up in thoughts like, "I DON'T WANNA GET UP TOMORROW." This is a complaint-free endeavor!

Before your date, gaze into the mirror and say, "I commit to giving you the kinds of magical life experiences you'll enjoy." Place a clear quartz somewhere on your person, and anoint yourself with a scent or color that makes you feel confident and enthusiastic. Then, as you have your date, sink into the experience. Allow your mind to go where it does; do not judge or dwell on thoughts. As you perform your date, state aloud your gratitude for life and your place in it.

When you return from your date, gaze in the mirror and thank yourself for setting and following through with this commitment as an act of love. You can also write out your experiences so that you can be motivated to do this on an ongoing basis.

Put Nature on a Pedestal

What a strange thing it is to feel the sting of unhappiness as a personal failure. For the most part, at no point in life does someone sit us down and say, "You have to be happy, and if you're not, you're failing." However, most people seem to carry this idea that a lack of happiness is them falling short in some way. How does that make any sense at all? Especially when your state of happiness is influenced so heavily by the context you exist in. Although there are things you can do on an individual level to embody joy and keep a positive mindset, which is likely to breed happiness, this battle is a lot less uphill if the environments and contexts you're in aren't completely awful. It's like the difference between running a race completely unfettered or with a fifty-pound sack of bricks on your back. Could you still get there? Yes, but your trip might require a lot more effort.

The world can be deeply unfair. Much of it has been built on greed and the shutting out of the natural world. Although there are unquestionable advances that make life infinitely safer and more comfortable, there are downsides. People are less likely to die of the elements, but the mental health of many has suffered from this strange space of modern society. People can simultaneously lack community and be more connected than ever.

Fortunately, you can create more circumstances of joy and opportunities for a great deal of happiness and purposefulness by deepening your appreciation for the natural world. Your ancestors were more in touch with nature and its gifts, as it was the environment in which they existed and found food, medicine, play, and entertainment. They felt the joy of its blessings.

In separating from this ecosystem that humans have built an artificial world upon, people have done themselves a great disservice for purposeful happiness. Witches understand the importance of appreciating Mother Nature and owning their place in this sacred circle of life. They nurture a connection to the land through reverent respect and strive to live collaboratively with it as active stewards.

It's time to take a cue from the craft and reclaim the deep sense of purpose, commitment, and pride that can be found through worshipping nature! While not everyone is the outdoorsy type, there is still a very clear link between spending time outside and individual well-being. Some studies suggest that spending as little as two hours in nature weekly can improve mood and provide a variety of physical health benefits. So even if you're not the type to slog out into the forest for hours before retreating home to pick off the ticks, you will still benefit from spending time in nature in more casual settings and holding it in the high esteem it deserves!

This planet is your home, and it should be respected and treated as a mother or elder. It deserves to be placed on a pedestal. If you are feeling burnt out and joyless, it may be a symptom of how modern life has separated you from your own personal connection to earth. Be kind to yourself and understand that this is a normal response to the abnormality of the modern context of the human species. At the same time, remember that you are a keeper of the land, and just how special and purposeful that is. Tap in to your magic and celebrate nature—get out there and start vibing with the land!

A Nature Altar

This activity will guide you in bringing a little of the great outdoors into your living space for purposeful connection and reverence.

Materials

- Natural items, such as rocks, sticks, live plants, flowers, rainwater, leaves, bones, shells, etc.
- A space to arrange your altar*
- Cleansing tools of your choice

*If you have kids or pets, set this up somewhere it won't be messed with. You can do this activity on your regular altar space or set up a different altar specifically for this purpose. The important thing is to be mindfully present during this activity.

Instructions

1. The first step to creating your nature altar is to collect the items. When you're out gallivanting in nature, pay attention to items that will "call" to you. If doing this is new to you, try not to overthink it. Just pay attention to items that you feel a tug or pull toward (I personally feel this in my chest and with an "opening" sensation behind my eyes).

2. When you see a rock or fallen twig that you fancy, ask if it is okay to take it and listen to the answer. You may "hear" the answer with your intuition or feel it in your body, or there may be an environmental cue (such as a gust of wind or bird calls).

3. Clear the chosen space for your altar and use a cleansing method of your choice. Scattering salt and using an altar spray are good methods.

4. Arrange your natural items on the altar in a way that feels right for you. This may take a few tries to get just right, but when you know, you'll know! You could try separating the space into quadrants to represent elements or seasons.

5. Spend time with your altar when you are feeling as if you could use a little grounding therapy. Gaze upon the objects and reflect on nature's cycles and your human place within them.

Connect with Earth Through Your Body and Breath

Many people feel some degree of insecurity when it comes to their body, particularly when it comes to body aesthetics. Although (most) people are not sat down and told explicitly that they don't measure up, they can see the bodies that get the leading roles in movies and appear on the magazine covers, and it speaks volumes without saying a thing. Additionally, somewhere along the line, a lot of people get their wires crossed when it comes to appearance, happiness, and self-worth. They can get caught up in this thinking trap that tells them their lives would be better if only they were a little thinner or a little more muscular, had a smaller nose, were shorter or taller, or had fewer bumps, wrinkles, or jiggly bits.

Here's the thing: Happiness is a state to be experienced, not a prize to be won. Can people find themselves happier after shifting something about their appearance? Sure, but this isn't the *requirement*. This body is how you navigate the world around you. It helps you move, it helps you survive, and it helps you experience your life. You can taste, touch, and dance under the moon. Your body gives you gifts of pleasure, pain, and the magic of your breath. Your body is a truly magical vessel, and this idea that you should hate it for not looking a certain way is such a barrier to getting the full experience and enjoyment out of life. You are of nature, and although you may not live fully immersed in her, you can still connect to the foundational principle of what it is to be alive in this amazing body, through nature and the healing portal of your breath.

Breathwork is a form of intentional breathing where breathing patterns are consciously altered for healing benefits. There are a variety of methods that you can learn; however, they all require the participant to pay conscious attention in manipulating their breath pattern for a specified length of time. Although it can be easy for some to dismiss breathwork as New Age BS, there's actually a great deal of scientific evidence that intentional breathing can have a variety of benefits, such as boosting immunity, decreasing anxiety, and helping people to work through emotions. Focusing on your breathing allows you to get out of the mental spirals you can get sucked into and get back to a grounded space within your body and on this earth. All in all, it's an amazing tool for wellness witchery!

There is so much life to be lived on the other side of self-hatred and disconnection from nature. Make peace with your physical form and use the power of it to make your life experience more connected and grounded.

A Body and Breathwork Practice

This practice can be used alone, or as part of other rituals and witchcraft practices, in order to form a powerful and deeply aligned connection with your body and the nourishing spirit of breath itself.

Materials

- Your own lungs
- A nature setting where you will be unlikely to be disturbed

Instructions

1. Sit with your back straight in a safe and comfortable position.

2. Begin breathing in through your nose and out through your mouth, paying attention to your natural breathing rhythm.

3. Place one hand on your chest and the other on your belly. Close your eyes and pay close attention to the sounds and scents of nature all around you.

4. Inhale through your nose for a count of four, pause, and then exhale through your mouth fully for at least seven counts.

5. Pay attention to how this breathing practice feels in your body. As you inhale, shift your thoughts toward gratitude for your breath. Breath is necessary for life, and when you strip away all the BS, you are left with the fact that you are beautifully alive. As you exhale, imagine all of your insecurities and hang-ups being expelled from your body to be cleansed by the earth and the air.

6. Continue this practice for up to five minutes for maximum benefit (always check in physically to make sure you aren't distressed).

7. When finished, open your eyes and thank your body for supporting you through this life. Thank nature for being your safe haven from mundane drudgery. Thank the air for the oxygen that sustains you. Thank yourself for taking the time to take care of yourself in this important and foundational way.

Let Your Animal Nature Out

As much as we may try to deny it in the "civilized" trenches of modern human life, we are animal creatures with animal needs. Indeed, you are a mammal with an incredible gift of consciousness, creativity, and emotion. This perfect marriage of wild and civilized! And although we humans have built our lifestyles somewhat distanced from more base instincts, that doesn't mean they cease to exist. Humans may be domesticated, but they still carry those impulses to fight, fornicate, and be free like their feral ancestors! By allowing yourself to connect with your animal nature, you can open the door to a very primal sort of joy.

Sensual pleasure is a prime example of the sort of juicy life experience that is denied all too often. And physical pleasure in a sexual sense isn't the only sensual pleasure that is denied. For every urge you suppress to run through the grass, dance in the breeze, or strip and hop into a lake, you are doing your spirit dirty! Embrace your sensuality, your divine nature, and the portal to pleasure that is your physical form. Pleasure is a part of life and should be integrated into your life experience.

Part of the reason the witch is such a compelling archetype in this world is because witches stay in their wild. They are simultaneously feared and revered for their unapologetic reclaiming of the human experience on their own terms, free of the limitations of polite society. Witches in popular media tend to be portrayed as either sexually uninhibited or unabashedly aging, both of which should simply be natural parts of being alive. Yet, in the context of societal ideals, both of these things seem equal parts alien and captivating.

You are meant to truly *experience* all that this life has to offer with your body, mind, and spirit. The more you insulate yourself from your primal desires and urges, the further you stray from joy. There are good reasons that you feel the call of the wild tugging at your heartstrings: You are a part of it, and it is a part of *you*. To interrupt the programming that has you believing you have to "fit in" and deny yourself the pure, carefree delight of being wild is to choose joy. It is an act of beautiful rebellion.

So soak up the sun, run free, engage in sex magic, and recognize the deep power of reclaiming your animal nature. Bask in the sensual glory of your wild.

A Sensual Ritual to Embrace Pleasure

This ritual is for reconnecting to pleasure in a joyful, nonjudgmental way. This can be challenging for those who have experienced trauma and/or shame in this domain, so make sure to check in with your needs and comfort level and adjust accordingly. Although sex magic can be uncomfortable at first, it can help provide an opportunity to heal some of these issues in a private and safe manner.

1. Find a private, safe space where you won't be bothered or interrupted.

2. Begin by setting an intention for what you are hoping to achieve. For example, if you are trying to heal your relationship with pleasure, set the intention to pursue pleasure with ease and to release any judgments about doing so.

3. Visualize what your fulfilled intention would look like, what it would feel like, and how doing such a thing would change you. Would life be simpler without such a hang-up? How would this open doors for you?

4. Set a relaxing mood with any music, lighting, or incense—whatever works for you. The intention here is to feel safe, calm, and carefree.

5. Begin exploring your body with your hands, and intentionally breathing. Keep your intention and the frequency it carries in the forefront of your mind. Use whatever method works for you to reach climax. This may look different for everybody: We are all different, with different needs!

6. As you feel that pleasure, keep your intention and picture in your mind as clearly as you can. Imagine all the energy you release through this act as "charging" this vision, helping to bring it to life.

If you are left with any residual guilt or shame after doing this, take some time to do some deep breathing, visualizing yourself exhaling away your hang-ups. Follow this by journaling or creating and repeating affirmations such as "I am worthy of pleasure and feeling good."

CHAPTER 3

Be Playful

Children often appear to enjoy life more than adults—this is likely based on their indulgent nature when it comes to spontaneity, play, and not yet being limited by social norms. At some point, we begin cutting ourselves off from our desires and impulses to take on the role of "functional grownup." However, everyone has the opportunity to turn away from this oppressive and limiting approach to life and open up to something different. Something more joyful. Magic can be your gateway to aligning yourself with a life that's more pleasurable and free. Reject the idea of adulthood being a dull container of responsibility and boredom and bring in the divine medicine of play to enjoy just how juicy life can be!

Because the witch strives to honor balance and harmony, they understand that fun is to responsibility as sleep is to waking life. These are complementary forces that both deserve a seat at the table; neither should be ignored. You were made to dance, to sing, to enjoy. You are meant to vibe in a state of amusement and bliss. In this chapter, you will use the craft to tap in to the frequency of joy by getting creative and honoring your inner child. The goal is to live with gusto, with magic as the door to a happier, more carefree life. It's time to break free, have fun, and *live*!

Engage In Dance Manifestation

When thinking of witchcraft, chances are the word doesn't conjure up a vision of chaotically dancing in your kitchen while almost burning the grilled cheese. However, this can actually be a big part of a witch's daily practice! I discovered the joy of dancing (poorly!) when rejecting the idea that people have to be good at something in order to do it. Sure, I may look like I'm getting electrocuted, but this ain't a ballroom competition and my skill level doesn't matter for what I'm trying to achieve: to purely catch a vibe, baby!

Movement is magic, and you can tap in to it regardless of your skill level. There is big, unbridled joy to be felt when you allow your body to move, to stretch, and to dance without inhibition. By tuning in to your body and allowing it to act as a channel for flow and positive energy, you are tapping in to something very powerful. This is why it feels so exhilarating to swing as high as you can, to run, and to dance, allowing your body to fully tune in to the frequency of joy.

Dancing became a part of my practice in the context of mirror work originally; however, once I saw how powerful it was for shifting and realigning my energy, it became one of my go-to methods for manifestation. As you learned earlier in this book, when manifesting, you aim to "feel into" the experience of already having your desire. You are trying to *mentally* and *energetically* step into alignment with your dreams and desires having already been fulfilled. Dance can be a really powerful way to make these energetic shifts, as it engages your physical body in a vibey and playful way, while leaving your mind free to dream up the reality you choose. This combo of using your body, your mind, and your energy can truly breathe life into your manifestations.

Now, any discussions about the magic of movement need to acknowledge that this looks different for different people, or even across the life span. Your mobility now, for instance, may look a lot different than it did in the past, and it may shift again in future years. Illness, disability, aging, and even mental health issues can all impact movement practices, so it's really important that you sidestep the urge to place judgments upon yourself and just work with what you've got. It's a beautiful thing to accept yourself for who you are in any given moment, free of comparisons and criticisms. This is something you deeply deserve.

So dance, witch, dance! Use your favorite carefree guilty pleasure jams to suck you out of a bad mood, and let your body be a physical channel for joy. Allow your mind to wander and explore all the delicious possibilities for the future, and let yourself move in flow without any expectation of performance. This is truly one of the most carefree pleasures you can give to yourself, and you should indulge in it often!

A Manifestation Dance Ritual

The following ritual can be performed any time (even multiple times per day!) as a method of powering your manifestations with sacred, joyous movement and flow. The key is to bring up the emotions desired and treat the movement as an act of generating power to your manifestations.

1. Begin by creating a "scene" of what you aim to manifest. I have found that the best way to do this is to pick a "mundane moment" after the manifestation is complete. For example, if you are trying to manifest buying a house, don't focus on getting the keys—focus instead on a scene of an ordinary day when you live there. The same goes for manifesting healing emotional states such as happiness: Instead of imagining a scene where it's just you but happier, pick a mundane moment that embodies that vision for you (e.g., waking up in bed feeling contented, as your kids crawl in for a Saturday morning snuggle).

2. Now put on some music that holds the frequency of what you are trying to call in. Most people have certain songs that evoke a specific vibe or emotion. You can keep these in your back pocket to be used to fast-track your alignment.

3. Put your music on and start dancing. As you begin to move, hold your scene in your head. What emotions are present in the scene? What is the environment? Lock in on the small, mundane details. Spin and move as if your physical action has the power to bring your scene to life. Let your motion and energy act as the power supply charging up your dreams!

Pencil In Intentional Joy

Have you experienced the feeling of completely dissociating from your own life? You might be suffering from a condition called *being a human in the modern era*!

Living mindfully and with intention is good medicine for this feeling of operating on autopilot. Although "intentional living" seems like just an *Instagram* buzz phrase, it's for a valid reason. This shit just feels *good*, and the best part is *it works*! Approaching your life in a way that is empowered and making moves that are in alignment with your values and desires is a great way to awaken your magic. This isn't just fluffy mysticism either (not that there's anything wrong with that!). Research has shown that using the power of intention can actually lead to brain changes, both in function and sometimes in structure by way of neuroplasticity.

So how can you use this tool to improve your happiness and well-being? Well, the first step is to understand the implications of such a thing. While most witches and mystics have a fairly good grasp of the power of mind over matter, there are still many folks who are sleeping on this gift. Acknowledging the power of your own attitudes and beliefs in flavoring this experience of life allows you to tap in to the ability to heal and shift so much even just within yourself—outside triggers be damned! This isn't to say that you can just declare yourself happy and then ride off into the sunset, but it *is* to say that you can choose to recognize the power of shifting your focus and begin to approach your life in a more empowered and purposeful way.

Although there are very real barriers to happiness that are not in your control, you can still empower yourself to shift your attention toward cultivating more joy and well-being. This isn't necessarily an easy task, but a skill to be cultivated. And it begins with teasing out what makes you happy and then choosing to make more space for these things on a daily basis. Just as you mentally pencil in time for brushing your teeth or showering, you should schedule in time to pursue the things that make you happy. Take the time to check in with yourself and ask, "What do I need right now? What can I do to shift my focus toward my own happiness?"

Imagine how your energy could benefit from even just five minutes a day of indulging your joy. This should be pushed as heavily as any hygiene practice and made to be seen as a top priority. Yes, life is busy, but if you can find the time to scroll through social media or look up ghost stories till 3 a.m. (guilty as charged!), then you can find the time to relentlessly pursue joy, for a few minutes at least. This idea that doing so would be frivolous or selfish is just another ridiculous limiting belief that deserves to be tossed into the trash. The practice of scheduling in joy, even if only for five minutes, is easy to do and can help shift your mood in a big way and invite in happiness. It also sends a signal to your subconscious that you are prioritizing your wellness, a deep and powerful act of self-love.

A "Five Minutes of Joy" Jar

The following activity is meant to ensure that when you have the time available to devote a few minutes to joy, you won't be spending it wringing your hands and wondering what to do. Instead, this activity will leave you equipped with a list of options to choose from that will enable your future self to hop right into the frequency of joy.

Materials

- A Mason jar
- Cleansing incense (copal, cedar, and frankincense are good options)
- 10–15 small rectangular strips of paper
- A pen

Instructions

1. Begin by cleansing your jar with the smoke from the incense. You can use any incense or herbal blend that is designed to cleanse.

2. On each strip of paper, write down one thing that brings you joy that you can do in five-minute intervals. Some ideas to get you started:
   - Listening to your favorite uplifting song
   - Writing a gratitude list
   - Creating silly haikus

- Watching something funny, like a video of a comedy routine
- Looking at old photos of a time when you were very happy
- Freewriting your daydreams
- Playing a game
- Doodling or painting
- Dancing
- Using your pendulum or tarot cards

3. Fold your strips of paper and place them in the jar.

4. Each day, pick a piece of paper from the jar and commit to doing the activity for five whole minutes to realign with joy.

Indulge Your Inner Child

No matter our age or maturity level, we all have an inner child who needs tending to. And just like regular children, they can be a channel for joy *and* a source of tantrum-y nonsense. Through inner child healing, you can get in touch with this little creature inside to open up to joy and to give yourself a little extra love and care. This is an integral shadow work practice for effective wellness witchery!

Childhood is a foundational time for development, with many picking up a lot of core beliefs about the self and the world during this time. Although childhood is typically a period associated with joy and play, the truth is that not everyone's childhood was a time of carefree fun. For a variety of reasons, many children end up dealing with trauma or growing up too soon, sustaining lasting wounds that can come up again and again throughout life. Basically, if your childhood was fraught with challenges, you might find yourself an adult with an inner child in need of tender care. Hell, even if your primary memories of being a kid are good ones, there may be some unhelpful lessons learned that need to be unlearned, and experiences that left a mark and need to be released.

The reality is that it can be really challenging to move with joy when you have a wounded inner child. Concepts like happiness and play may feel wholly unfamiliar to you if you have never felt them before. Giving yourself permission to play and succumb to joy may even feel completely foreign. This is totally normal and okay!

It's important to be gentle with yourself and to be open to the possibility that you have immense power to give *yourself* the loving space to play and heal. Witchcraft can be a really effective self-care tool to tackle this kind of healing. Inner child shadow work allows you to establish a relationship with this buried part of yourself and ask, "What is it that you need? How can I help you?"

Often, your triggers and sore spots as an adult have some root in your early developmental years. This is why you can sometimes even surprise *yourself* when you lash out, become insecure or jealous, or struggle to hold on to big things when you feel undeserving. Although you might feel silly as an adult taking time to connect with your inner child, it can be immensely important to do so in order to tackle and heal these root issues and stop them from continuing to impact your life. And even if your childhood was amazing, it can still be beneficial to connect with your inner child, keeping the joy and play alive in your adult life.

Ultimately, you cannot change the things that happened to you; however, you *do* have the power to shift your future. The way you do this isn't by bypassing your traumas or your wounds but by sitting with them, acknowledging them, and holding space for that tender little unruly creature that may not have gotten the love and attention they needed in the past. Hold space for that wounded child to play, and lavish them in the love that they need to heal. After all, you are worthy, you've always been worthy, and you deserve it!

Herbal Play Dough for Invoking Your Inner Child

This lavender (for calm) and rose (for love) infused dough is for indulging your inner child to come out and play. You can do practically anything with this dough. You can create with it, you can smush it up, you can write secrets in it before kneading them back into oblivion—whatever your inner child needs! The one thing you should always do is affirm to yourself that you are safe. Inner child work can be triggering and emotional, so use whatever emotional/spiritual protection methods work for you to be comfortable.

Materials

- 1 cup all-purpose flour
- ½ cup salt
- 2 tablespoons cream of tartar
- 2 tablespoons grapeseed oil
- 6 drops lavender essential oil
- 6 drops rose essential oil
- 1 cup hot water
- A few drops food coloring (optional)

Instructions

1. Mix the flour, salt, and cream of tartar together in a medium bowl.

2. In a separate small bowl, mix together the grapeseed and essential oils.

3. Add the oils to the dry mix and blend.

4. Add the hot water and food coloring if you choose to use some (I typically use 2 or 3 drops each of blue and red). Mix.

5. Knead the hell out of it! In order to get that prime consistency, you must go hard on this step. If you have any pent-up bitch-slappy energy, this is your time to shine!

6. Once your dough is complete, you can use it while connecting with your inner child, whatever that looks like for you. Between uses, keep the dough in a sealed airtight bag at room temperature.

Get Lost in a Daydream

Witches love visualization because we recognize the power of conjuring something up using just the mind's eye. After all, this is the seed of all things! Ideas and creativity are birthed in the imagination, coming to life once you've pondered them enough to give them form. Your coffee maker was just an idea once, as were your smartphone and most of your life decisions! Once you awaken to how powerful the mind can be, you begin to see how you can harness it to create a life experience you love.

In a world full of busyness and distraction, daydreaming has become a lost art. However, daydreaming (the aimless drifts in consciousness where you float away from the chaos of reality) is a necessary tool for joy. When you take the time to vibe in the imagination space, possibilities are boundless, and you give yourself the gift of experiencing your biggest hopes, dreams, and desires—even though they haven't technically happened yet. Additionally, you open up the doors to creativity, as the aimless mind can be a powerful generator. And in terms of manifesting, daydreaming allows you to align with your highest selves, in your brightest and most unlimited futures.

Although daydreaming is seen as a normal part of life in the earlier years, people certainly don't prioritize it in adulthood. As a grownup, you may treat daydreaming as you treat other forms of aimless creativity and joy-seeking activities: as something frivolous and low on the priority list. This is a big mistake! You would be happier as an individual (and humans would be happier collectively as a species) if you made a point of daydreaming more often, reaping the rewards of allowing your mind to fantasize and freely wander. Daydreaming can be just the kind of mini-vacation from reality that adults so sorely need!

So let's normalize daydreaming across the life span! Rather than getting sucked into the vortex of modern distractions (social media, watching TV, and thinking of all the ways you could be doing "more"), let's get back to a place where daydreaming is seen as a necessary part of life. You need to first give your mind the space and permission to wander, and to get acquainted with the feeling of unlimited possibility, in order to conjure up the magic this practice holds. It's all too easy to slip into the belief that your dreams are too big or too unrealistic. Whether it's intentional or not, you are likely familiar with the feeling of putting a ceiling on your own imagination and creativity. Well, with all due respect, this is a resounding *fuck that*!

What the world truly needs is more dreamers, more imagination, and less limiting BS! Even if your life feels more chaotic than calm, allow yourself to drift into the space where all things are possible and get familiar with the feeling of all your wishes being fully within reach. Give this gift to yourself, as it is certainly not going to be gifted to you from *out there*.

A Daydreaming Bath Ritual

This ritual will help you shuck off the limitations of the predictably mundane and tap in to the magic of the untethered mind. It is best done on or around the new moon, or in the early waxing phase when the moon is not yet illuminating the sky.

Materials

- 1½ cups Epsom salts
- A citrine crystal
- A purple candle

Instructions

1. Begin by running a warm bath, adding Epsom salts to the water to dissolve.

2. Place your citrine crystal by the side of your tub, near where your head will be.

3. Place your candle on the counter or a nearby table (somewhere stable and safe!). Light it, stating out loud, "Let this be the spark of unlimited imagination."

4. Get into the tub and breathe deeply, allowing yourself to relax fully, both body and mind.

5. Let your mind wander wherever it chooses to go. As with meditation, just observe your thoughts rather than place judgments on them. If they veer off in too negative a direction, try to think of things you feel hopeful about or things you desire. If your brain tries to come up with reasons why these things are not possible, open your eyes and focus on your candle flame, visualizing it as the spark of unlimited imagination.

6. When you have done this, thank yourself for giving yourself the time to daydream: This is a gift!

7. Take your citrine crystal and carry it on your person for the week after your bath, or hold it whenever you feel like you could use a daydream.

Aim for Loud and Carefree

As I get older, I'm frequently surprised and delighted by the lack of fucks I have to give about what other people are going to think of me. This is a very welcome development that many people note as they age. A lot of people can struggle at times, particularly in their younger years, with people-pleasing and spending far too long not living authentically in an attempt to be accepted. The problem with orienting yourself in such a direction is that you set yourself up to fail every time. When you consider how widely varied people's personalities and values can be, it's obvious that this is an impossible task. The only thing guaranteed in such a scenario is making yourself miserable and making life harder. Think of it this way: If you're already feeling tapped out by the stressors of this grown-up life, why drain even more of your precious energy by suppressing your own authenticity?

Most people are aware of a deep longing to live in a way that feels free. Free of judgment and shame, and free of the limitations placed on you by yourself and by others. This is where witches shine. Even to claim the title of "witch" is to step into freedom, when you consider the unnecessary baggage the term can carry for those intent on misunderstanding what witchcraft is. This may be part of the reason that witches can be so triggering and compelling. To stand firm in your truth as a connected and spiritual being is a powerful act of breaking the mold and becoming free.

Although Western culture tends to view treating the pursuit of your own happiness and truth as a selfish act, it should actually be seen as an act of service for those around you. The energy you bring to your life and relationships when you allow yourself to simply be *you* is some top-tier magic! Being unapologetically yourself is a gift. Though it may not feel that way on those days when the inner critic is loud and belligerent, it is true.

Here are some facts that aren't stressed enough in modern society:

- You deserve to be yourself, freely.

- You deserve to be surrounded by people who love you for who you truly are, and to reap the rewards of authentic friendships.

- You deserve to be your biggest, boldest, most carefree self!

You've likely had experiences meeting people who are just so carefree in their own authenticity that they are practically magnetic. Even if you don't necessarily agree with or even *like* these people, you can still identify with feeling a little in awe of their ability to just show up and be transparent in their own truth. Well, the good news is that you have this ability, too, and by choosing to move your focus toward nurturing this shift, you can summon a life full of ease and aligned joy!

To be honest, it will take some deprogramming to get to a place where authenticity in a public sense can feel safe. "Fake it till you make it" is a legitimate strategy and can act as your "training wheels" during the beginning of this journey, when being yourself may not feel safe or comfortable. *Persist!*

Although tackling the fear and discomfort might make you want to crawl out of your skin, it really doesn't take that long until it starts to feel easier, and from there it just snowballs until you hit your stride. You will know it when you feel it: It's big, empowered magic.

So no more dimming yourself or your dreams in order to fit in or make other folks comfortable! Aim to be your biggest self in order to align with joy! This is "go big or go home" energy that shouldn't be toned down. Your unique quirks are fun and authentic and not to be shucked off to please someone else. Live boldly, laugh loudly, chase your dreams unapologetically, and do whatever makes you smile.

The Audacity Spell

The following spell is to give a magical boost of confidence to step up as your brightest, most audacious self:

Materials

- Cleansing tools of your choice
- A yellow candle
- Himalayan pink salt (enough to fill bowl halfway)
- A small bowl
- A bay leaf
- A Sharpie
- Sparkles
- Multicolored sprinkles

Instructions

1. Open up your space for magic and cleanse yourself and your materials.

2. Light your candle and gaze into it, thinking about what it would feel like to have the brazen audacity to show up to your life just the way you want. What would that look like? Is it far off?

3. Put the salt in the bowl.

4. On the bay leaf, write "THE AUDACITY" with the Sharpie.

5. Crumble the bay leaf onto the salt, imagining that as it crumbles, so too do any barriers keeping you from showing up as your biggest, boldest self. State out loud, "May I have the audacity to step into my life as who I truly am. May I have the strength to prioritize myself. May I step into my joy and my power."

6. Sprinkle the sparkles in the bowl. You might be thinking it's a little silly or ridiculous to be using sparkles for a serious spell, but that is precisely the point: to show the joy of a little flashy razzle-dazzle and how it can remind you to be your true, quirky self.

7. Now add the sprinkles to the bowl, and admire this ridiculous, fun little bowl of chaos you just created!

8. Drip a drop of candle wax into the middle of the bowl to complete the spell.

9. Place this spell on your dresser or somewhere you will see every morning. When you look at the sprinkles and sparkles and the intentions you set, let the spell be a reminder to be your biggest, boldest self. Be as sparkly and chaotic as you wanna be. You only have one life: Live it loud and carefree!

Treat Your Life As an Experience

Life has a way of relentlessly churning, the gears moving at a speed that's both agonizing and dizzying. I'm often left thinking that if I could only pause it for a while to "catch up," then I'd be set—I'd be able to get ahead of it and sort my shit out in such a way that I'd never have to feel as if I were being chewed up within its spokes again.

This is a common limiting belief held up in modern life. We get sucked up into the chaos of trying to *do it all*, and it feels as if taking care of ourselves and setting ourselves up for success is an impossibility ("There's just no time!"). The side effect of living like this is that we become numb, touched out, and our days begin to blur into one big, empty-feeling struggle. This is life on autopilot, complete with a deep aching desire in our chests to *wake up already*!

The thing they don't teach in school is that life is meant to be *lived*; it's meant to be an *experience*. There's truly no other way to approach self-care in a system that leaves so little time for yourself. You have to get sneaky about it, which means collecting tiny bits of magic in shifts while you keep one foot in the mundane. You have to honor the moments as the experiences they are. As opportunities brimming with potential to be magic.

So light a candle while you clean. Dress up nice for your kitchen and dance like the unhinged creature that you are. Take a minute to breathe, to pause, and to use the fancy stuff you've been saving for a special occasion. *Your life* is the occasion, your happiness is the goal, and your impulses and quirks are there to guide you toward a happier and more joyous life.

Living in a mindful way is the secret sauce to treating your life as an experience. You grow up thinking you have to look and behave in X, Y, and Z ways in order to be a functional grownup, but how are you really going to live your life in a prescriptive, orderly way if you want to be free? Kids follow their urges to walk in the grass and jump in the waves—to truly experience each moment of life—and yet grow up and ditch this freedom in favor of an adulthood of feeling perpetually asleep at the wheel.

Not anymore.

Know this: If the funky socks make you feel joy, then *wear them*. If wrapping your hands around a hot cup of tea makes your heart expand, then *do it*. Your mind and your spirit are your own; nobody can peek in on them, so take those sneaky moments of joy throughout the day and *claim them*. Those wild impulses you have to pull over and crunch in the leaves or sniff that tree are there for a reason. Life is to be lived—make sure yours is a whole experience. Incredible experiences are hidden in your small tasks, and they are waiting for you to come and bask in them. Do the next thing that feels right and wade in the feelings that wash over you. Happiness isn't an "aha" moment; it's woven in as an available path in all moments. Shake up to wake up!

A Vibey Tea Ritual

This ritual is a witchy way to bask in the sensory experience of your life. It is best done in a situation where you will not be disturbed or interrupted, as it is a mindfulness exercise. To make dedication candles, I personally use tea lights that have been dressed in oils and/or herbs for some specific purpose, and then only light each candle when I'm doing the specific thing. For this ritual, my candle is dressed in lavender, chamomile, and jasmine and is saved for this activity alone.

Materials

- A small candle that is dedicated to this purpose
- Water (enough to fill a teacup)
- A bag of calming herbal tea
- A teacup
- 1 teaspoon honey

Instructions

1. Begin by lighting your candle and taking some deep breaths in through your nose and out through your mouth to anchor you into the moment.

2. Boil the water and place the tea bag in your cup. Continue intentionally breathing.

3. Once your water is boiled, pour it into your cup to steep your tea. Gaze at it while it brews—no scrolling through your phone or doing busywork. This is structured mindfulness, so although you may feel uncomfortable in doing this, it is an essential practice that will help your cause.

4. Stir the honey into your cup clockwise, stating an intention to sweeten your perspective toward sinking into every moment. Watch as the honey melts into your cup. Imagine melting into every moment like this.

5. Sit (move your candle with you if you need to move to find a seat) and hold your cup between your palms when the cup has cooled enough to safely do so. Feel the heat of your cup on your palms. Notice it and how you feel. Are you relaxed?

6. Now feel the steam rising toward your face, carrying the scent of the tea.

7. Drink, and as you do, pay attention to the feeling of the hot liquid moving down your throat. This is a particularly unique sensory experience that people tend to take for granted, which is a shame! These are the sorts of everyday sensory experiences that allow you to live deliciously, should you turn your attention toward them.

Create Just for the Sake of It

We humans have this bonkers preoccupation with keeping busy: We treat it as if it's a virtue to work yourself into the ground to avoid sitting with your own thoughts. However, big magic can be found in the sleepy corners of your life. When we neglect to leave room for the unstructured, we operate in the frequency of control and resistance, which is certainly not the vibe for a contented life! Part and parcel to this is the notion that we aren't *doing* enough. This is the curse of brain-led thinking, which places negative value judgments on aimlessness. Immediately when we sit to even do purposeful "nothing" (for example, meditating or reflecting in gratitude), our brains cannot abide it and switches us into busy mode. And it's not even *useful* busy either—this hunk of skull meat would have us just pick up the phone to scroll into the void just for the sake of avoiding being idle. Witchcraft allows you to challenge these sorts of limiting beliefs and summon up happiness through stillness, connection, and seeking opportunities to lean way into creativity and joy.

Artists and witches alike are aware of the secret here, which is that aimless creativity is necessary for purposeful creating. As a writer, half my job to get words on the page is to sit in the quiet with myself, ignoring the desperate screams of my brain, which doesn't want to give up the wheel. This is as necessary and fundamental a part of the process as putting pen to paper. And any attempts to justify it to yourself as neglectful or foolish don't make that fact lose power. Just as sleep is a necessary part of life, so too is doing nothing a necessary part of doing *anything*.

When was the last time *you* gave yourself structured permission to be creative just for the sake of it? This is another prime example where you can take your cue from children. In childhood, creativity and play are considered paramount to healthy development, whereas in adulthood you tend to hold them at arm's length unless they can generate income or gain you some kind of social favor. This creates a situation where the creativity itself is not incentivized, but the *outcome* of that creativity is. In many cases this can lead to things like creative blocks and burnout because you essentially exploit this beautiful dimension of the human spirit by assigning success to the result rather than to the process. And it's the process that reaps more rewards!

Your happiness assignment is this: Go forth and create. Create something shitty! Create something and leave it unfinished! Create a masterpiece! To hell with the outcome: *Just create!*

Aimless creativity is seen as offensive to the culture of producing things, and thus, to create just for the joy of doing so is to essentially take your power back. It's a reclamation of spirit! Indulge in aimless creativity to find joy and play. Not everything needs to be a means to an end; make art just for the sake of it, no expectations attached.

A Free-Painting Spell

The following spell is an exercise in approaching creativity with no expectations other than for the fulfillment that comes from creating. There are some magical additions included to make it a vibey and spiritual expression to nourish your witchy soul.

Materials

- Some chill, vibey music
- The anointing oil made in "A Recipe and Ritual to Hack Your Senses" in Chapter 1
- A carnelian crystal
- Some watercolor or acrylic paint
- A canvas or large sheet of paper
- Some moon water or rainwater*

*Clean moon water or rainwater can be used for this to rinse your brushes and dilute your paint. You are free to use regular water if you want; however, this just adds another dimension of witchy connectedness to this practice.

Instructions

1. Begin by assessing your mood. This spell is to give yourself the structured permission to create for *no other reason* than to create. The outcome is not important; performance is not the metric by which we measure success with this task. This is about finding joy through the creative process itself.

2. Choose your colors accordingly: Are you vibing with how you feel now, or are you calling in the energy of something better? If you're looking for a little color magic inspiration, start here:

   - Red: passion, love, intensity
   - Yellow: happiness, joy, optimism

- Green: growth, prosperity, health
- Blue: wisdom, peace, psychic energy

3. Put on your music. What you choose is not as important as why you are choosing it. The purpose is to help you get into a flowy creative state!

4. Take your anointing oil from Chapter 1 and apply it to your body. You can experience resistance with engaging in unstructured creativity, so make yourself more comfortable with this part of the process by hacking into your senses using the oil.

5. Take your carnelian crystal and hold it between your palms. Walk in a circle around the perimeter of your workspace and affirm that you are opening it up to creativity. The type of aimless creativity that exists simply for fun expression. Your work is under no obligation to look presentable or be done well. The task itself is the goal.

6. Take your paint and canvas (or paper) and get to work. Move to the music and allow yourself to just flow in the moment. Being fully present for this is much more important than doing a good job or creating anything of value. This is the magic of creatively tapping in to happy.

Make Your Life a Performance Art Piece

In life, you are constantly performing. You have different faces you show to different people. Your clothing is performance, as is the way you behave in public. Your public declarations of who you align with and why put on a show about who you are and what you stand for. How you present yourself online is typically staged and curated to some degree. Performance doesn't have to have a connotation of being fake or bad, it just *is*. You can be authentic and yet still be putting on a show. It's just the way you show up to life!

That being said, you do perform in ways that don't serve you. From an early age, many pick up the bad habit of masking their true selves to please other people and fit in. This includes behaviorally conforming to align with social norms, which can leave a lot of unbridled joy untouched on the table. Then, once you get out there into the great big world of adulthood, you aren't encouraged to chase play, creativity, and the brazen pursuit of happiness the way that you did when you were a kid. You perform the role of "responsible adult." This is a travesty, and it's up to you to get back to a place where you pursue joy and ease with the enthusiastic vigor and selfishness that is needed in order to thrive and manifest lasting happiness.

You have but one magical life, and it should be lived on your terms! In youth it can seem especially easy to simply put these masks on and carry out the business of being a person; however, in your later years it becomes abundantly clear what an oppressive burden this is. This is why many folks embark on some sort of journey to desperately deprogram themselves from this in their later years, beginning the messy unraveling process of trying to figure out who they even are. This is necessary and good, however uncomfortable it can feel. It is shadow work in action, the witch's great work of healing themselves and unearthing who they want to be, free of affairs and limitations!

Life should be a performance in the sense that it should be creative, messy, and emotive. Chase your joy, witch! You are here for just a limited time, so you should aim to live so big and free that it entertains you, even in the less joyful moments (*especially* then). The goal is to operate in a state of ease and flow, living life in a way that feels authentic, easy, and *good*. Live your life as a performance art piece—a beautiful expression of your authenticity and alignment with joy!

It doesn't matter if your thing is to cosplay as a pirate, cover yourself in tattoos, or dance in the street. The important thing is to abandon the mental baggage that would have you dimming your ten-thousand-watt brilliance to conform to social norms that don't prioritize happiness anyways. You deserve to be happy; it is your right to live as loudly and as freely as you choose. So dance while you clean, sing loudly in the shower. The performance of you being *you* will not only serve your own best interests but will also provide an example to those who haven't yet found the courage to tackle this themselves!

A Joyful Salt and Energy Cleanse

The following spell is to cleanse and shift the energies that would have you asleep to your own magic. It will help you to call in your dream role: the thriving star of your own story!

Materials

- 4 small bowls
- Salt (enough to fill each bowl)
- 4 pinches marjoram

Instructions

1. Pick a room of your house where you will be free to sing loudly without judgment, fear, or shame.

2. Fill your bowls with the salt and add a pinch of marjoram to each for happiness. Place one bowl in each of the four corners of the room to soak up any stank, negative energy.

3. In the center of the room, ground and center yourself. State aloud your commitment to yourself to shamelessly pursue your joy, and ask to be free of the fears and limiting beliefs that would have you keep yourself small to fit in some ridiculous box. Breathe deep, visualizing your exhales as releasing these limitations to be absorbed by the salt in the corners of the room.

4. When you feel ready, begin to sing as loudly as you can. This doesn't need to be good, or even a proper song. This is truly a "you do you" moment. The important thing is to drop any inhibitions or insecurities about doing so. This is your practice to be as loud, as carefree, and as unhinged as you choose. The world will continue to spin, I promise!

5. As you sing, dance or do whatever else it is that will bring you into the feeling of being joyfully, exhilaratingly free! This is good practice for building up the confidence to bring this energy to the world at large!

6. Leave the salt in the corners of the room for three days, and commit to doing this practice at least once a day for those three days. If you choose to commit to doing this for longer, simply replace the salt and herbs in the bowl so they are fresh.

CHAPTER 4

Be Still

Chasing happiness isn't always action in motion. Sometimes you need to sit in reflection, in peace, and hold space for the shadow to find the light. Joy is not spontaneously born—a random ignition of positive vibes—but rather something that emerges as a result of integrating all the frequencies of the human experience. In the modern context of meme culture, people are simultaneously told to think positive, but not *too* positive or that would be toxic! The truth, like most truths, lies somewhere in the middle. A balance of action and stillness.

Witches embrace the important responsibility of personal mastery when it comes to mindset and opening up to possibilities that are beyond what the current reality supports. Most importantly, they recognize the importance of this balance between *doing* and *not doing*, and the sacred gift of personal empowerment that comes with it. In order to move in alignment with your heart and your happiness, you need to make space to sit in stillness and listen to the magic within. This is the shadow side of big action—the quieter, more introspective aspect of propelling yourself into a happier reality. In this chapter, you will practice the quieter work of the craft, the solitary weaving and healing needed to invite boundless joy.

Sit with Your Feelings

Unpleasant emotions are a part of the daily experience. Feelings like fear, anger, sadness, and grief are constants in an ever-changing life; however, most aren't taught how to hold them, and the discomfort they create within often feels like too much to bear. In modern Western society, we are taught instead to seek out quick-fix solutions, and as a result we tend to rush these big feels out the door as quickly as possible or try to ignore them. Whether we use food, spending, substances, problematic behaviors, or straight-up run-of-the-mill avoidance, our typical strategies seem to be anything to avoid *feeling the thing* itself. When you consider that these painful feelings are such a profound and large part of your emotional world, it's no wonder that lacking the ability to sit with them can lead to more challenges down the road. It doesn't need to be this way....

True, these big, scary feelings can feel chaotic and difficult to control. They're fiery—but as with fire, there is the option of both destruction *and* transformation. When you are equipped to hold them, you allow yourself to be a responsible fire wielder. Through witchcraft, you can direct the energy in a way that has the power to heal and transform rather than burn and destroy. Alternatively, when you struggle to bear their heat, you are depriving yourself of your ability to turn them into power. Feeble attempts to soothe them without actually dealing with them are akin to pissing on a house fire, with similar efficacy.

Your first step to creating power from emotion has been awakening to the necessity of sitting with hard feelings. But what does sitting with them look like in practice? The method would vary depending on the person; however, at a base level, it starts with the ability to literally *sit* with them. Resist the urge to busy yourself or text your friends. Resist the urge to feed them that which would only deplete you in the long run, whether it be sugar, alcohol, or something else.

Just sit. Breathe. Feel.

Observe the feeling of wanting to crawl out of your own skin, allowing yourself to let it wash over you without succumbing to avoidance. Where do you feel it in your body? Sink into the moment and take inventory of which body systems and sensations are activated. What's the temperature? Does it have a color? Allow your mind to plead its case for avoiding this discomfort while you carry on, just as you would continue to bandage up a shrieking injured child. In doing so, you are doing yourself a great service. The more capable you are of holding your heavy feelings, the more resilient you become. Lift rather than bury. Flex your emotive muscles.

Although this is a worthy skill for everyone to learn, you should also be realistic about the importance of safety when grappling with these hard things. Use affirmations, calming stones, or whatever method you choose in order to feel safe and grounded when working with something so serious and powerful. If your big, scary feelings are the result of trauma or other emotionally scarring conditions, your safety is especially important. This might mean doing these sorts of practices with a therapist or medical professional, and that's okay. There should be no placing judgments on your healing. You do what you must to push through, and you celebrate yourself for it!

Feelings are adaptive; they help form the rich tapestry of the human experience. In order to truly thrive, you must trade in avoidance and fear for self-understanding and adaptability.

Cloud Dough for Working Through Difficult Feelings

The following practice serves to help you work through your emotions. It can be incredibly difficult to sit with your feelings when they are painful and the call to move on to doing something more comfortable hits the soul like a scream! Busying your hands with something tactile, like cloud dough, can make it easier to remain present and focused. This recipe uses lavender essential oil for calm and blue food coloring for serene color magic.

Materials

- ½ cup gentle unscented lotion
- A few drops blue food coloring
- A few drops lavender essential oil
- A medium bowl
- 1 cup cornstarch
- Cleansing tools of your choice

Instructions

1. Mix the lotion, food coloring, and essential oil in the bowl until thoroughly combined.

2. Add the cornstarch and mix well.

3. Take your dough and begin kneading it until it takes shape and becomes smooth. Set aside.

4. Cleanse yourself and your area with the method of your choosing, focusing on getting to an energetic state that feels safe and calming.

5. Sit beside your dough and allow yourself to feel your feelings, reminding and affirming to yourself that you are safe.

6. As you sit with your feelings, start to roll, knead, and squish the cloud dough in your hands. If you get the urge to resist your emotions and check your phone or whatever, just keep those fingers moving. If it helps to knead the dough in front of the body part that is feeling the pain as a symbolic representation of moving through it, then do that. Your method can and should be unique and personal to you.*

*It's important to note that this practice may take as little as two minutes or it may take an hour or more. It is very possible that, to begin with, you may only be able to tolerate the powerful emotions for a short period. Like any skill, it takes practice! Be gentle with yourself and trust your own guidance.

Allow Less to Be More

Advertising is fascinating, because it shows you a deep glimpse into the core of the human condition. In order to be sold to, you are presented first with your problems, then a proposed "solution" (the product), followed by the triumphant outcome. Advertisers know that *this* is the secret sauce: the "after" photo, the desired outcome that's fairly consistent across the board, a happier you! And they depict this via the actors on screen twirling gleefully in a sort of joyful caricature.

Witches know better.

Although there are many actions you can take to be happier, to constantly be chasing happiness in the "doing" is to ignore half the equation. This is like if you consistently chose to neglect sleep for more waking hours, holding a personal motto of "I'll sleep when I'm dead." It wouldn't take long for your life and your well-being to meet the consequences. There needs to be balance! Despite the prevailing notion that the tricky business of becoming happier is a marathon run of *doing all the things*, there is big work done in the quiet stillness. This quiet work is what complements the action, allowing you to find a more robust and holistic form of happiness at the end of the road.

As counterintuitive as it may seem, there is big action in rest. Much like your body and brain are nourished by rest as you sleep, prioritizing stillness in your waking hours can be equally beneficial. It's the perfect antidote to a society that incentivizes doing too much. For us witches, it's no secret that rest is not just a way for us to bounce back from doing the work: It is an incredibly foundational piece *of the work itself*.

The desire to be happier is often motivated by wanting to show up to the world in a way that feels more "complete." You want to parent better, you want to understand yourself better, you want to be healed.

So why do so many still feel like rest is something selfish?

If you are wanting to heal, you need to vibe in the stillness and unravel the tangled-up bits. If you are wanting to respond to others better, you have to sit alone with yourself and explore your reactions in the past. If you want to connect with your inner guidance, you need to make time to shut down the brain chatter in order to truly hear that guide. If you want to work through painful emotions, you've got to give them an audience and find out what they're trying to tell you. *Selfish is not always a bad thing.* You are allowed to do self-serving things that make you feel better just because—period! So the next time you catch yourself resisting rest, fight back.

Rest can be action and is powerful medicine. It can help you draw lines of protection around yourself. And it is the channel through which you can connect to yourself.

Take a moment to think about just how much rest can do for you and how you show up for the world. Think about your feelings toward rest, reflection, and intentionally just *be*-ing at any given time point. Is it comfortable for you or not? Can you take the time to sit in quiet reflection?

A Bathing in Quiet Reflection Meditation

The following is a structured practice to approach stillness and reflection—to doing "nothing" as a form of self-care.

Materials

- 10 drops rose essential oil
- 10 drops peppermint essential oil
- 1½ tablespoons carrier oil (such as olive, grapeseed, or sweet almond)
- 2 small bowls
- 1 cup powdered whole milk
- ½ cup baking soda
- A candle
- Cleansing tools of your choice

Instructions*

1. Mix the essential oils and carrier oils in one bowl.
2. Mix the milk and baking soda in the other bowl.
3. Mix the oils into the dry mixture.
4. Run your bath.
5. Add a hefty scoop of the mix to your bathwater and let it dissolve. (If there is any mix left over, put it in a sealed jar and keep in a dry place for up to a month.)
6. Light the candle and do an energetic cleanse with smoke, sound, or whichever method feels best for you.

7. Get undressed and get into the water. Take a few full, deep, intentional breaths in through your nose and out through your mouth to begin, then let your mind begin to wander. There's no need to direct your thoughts too much; the purpose of this is mainly to train yourself to sit in quiet reflection. Allow whatever comes up to come up, and then let it go and continue sitting in reflection.

*For an added magical boost, perform this meditation during the introspective energy of the new moon.

Savor Your Life

I'd like to consider myself a reasonable person, but I go from zero to ballistic pretty quickly when put in a position where I have to exercise even the slightest bit of patience. Although this is something for me personally to work on, it's also a reflection of the cushy world that I happened to grow up in. Quick-fix solutions and instant gratification have become such a normalized part of life that patience, a thing that can already be hard enough, becomes even more so.

Although practicing patience can feel agonizing, you can gain a deeper appreciation for life by leaning into making yourself wait and savoring the moments in between. Because your life *should* be savored! Your precious time here should be experienced to the fullest in pursuit of happy, joyful living. You should resist the urge to hate on waiting, reducing it to just a necessary evil blocking the path to the things you want. Instead, you should see it as an opportunity to grow! Waiting will *always* be there; it's your response to it that dictates whether it depletes your pleasure or adds to it.

The witch's path often leads to activities that teach patience. For example, gardening herbs for your spells can teach you how to savor the waiting phases of life as you plant the seeds, nurture them, and then reap the rewards (which cannot always be rushed). Creating a spell jar made with the flowers you nurtured from seed just hits different. It helps you get *invested* in the outcome. Slow herbalism is another example that will be familiar to the witch—waiting for a plant in the wild to be ready to be ethically harvested, then preparing it and letting it slowly infuse for an oil or tincture (a process that can take literal months) before seeing your labor pay off. It's the perfect counter for a culture that's been captured by convenience.

And the truth is that a lot of the convenience we enjoy in a quick-fix culture comes at a high price. In many cases it costs the integrity of this beautiful planet, as people engage in short-sighted practices that are unfriendly to the ecosystem. It can also cost knowledge, as we trade in self-sufficiency skills for the hands-off convenience comforts of modernity. And it costs happiness, as it becomes normalized to want things *now*, not fully respecting that waiting and working toward things is a normal part of life rather than some wretched inconvenience that's meant to separate us from our desires.

Although it can seem like self-imposed torture to grow a plant from seed when you can go to the market and grab a fully grown plant today, the point is the intention—the deliberate effort to bring something into existence that wasn't there before. The point is the process, be it slow and be it maddening, that can teach you important things about the value of your time and efforts. The point is seeing that there is a lot of juicy life, learning, and feelings that occur in the meanwhile of waiting for something to blossom into fruition, guided by your will and by your hands.

Sometimes fulfillment is happiness in disguise!

If you want to unfurl a bit of happiness that feels outside your grasp, you must reject the tendency to long for instant gratification and quick fixes. Instead, lean into making yourself wait, and cultivate simple pleasure in dancing with the feelings of anticipation.

An Herbal Practice in Patience

One simple way to lean into the pleasure of waiting for something you've nurtured with your intentions is to try growing your own herbs from seed. Rosemary, garden sage, and thyme are a few simple magical herbs that are fairly easy to grow from seed, even in small spaces such as windowsills. Plant the seeds with the following incantation: "From root to leaf, I nurture your growth, fed by my love and tended with my patience." For an added boost, put a cleansed green calcite crystal in the pot.

To make this process even more fun and immersive, sketch pictures of your seedlings' progress in a sketchbook or journal. This is to help you find creative joy in all aspects of the plant's life cycle, not just the enjoyment of the finished plant itself.

Once your plant is grown, you can use its leaves and sprigs in various spells and rituals, adding a deeply personal magical boost to your workings.

Indulge In Power-Saving Mode

For many, a huge barrier to happiness is this tendency to glamorize doing the *most*. We want to work hard, do a good job, become better people and better parents, and try to keep up with those around us as well as our own expectations. At some point on our journey to be a functional human, we've deeply absorbed the notion that in order to be of value, we have to be achieving at a scale that's both unrealistic and unsustainable.

I urgently call on you to lower your expectations and *hit that power-save button*!

In the age of empowerment memes, taking time off from doing as a form of self-care is becoming a popular sentiment. But what does this actually mean, and how can doing this help you to show up to your life in a way that amplifies your happiness and magic?

You know that rest is an effective antidote for stress and overwhelm; however, there are various ways to rest. Naps, mental health days, and having cereal for dinner are all wonderful rebellions against this pressure to do too much. So is simply saying, "Screw the to-do list," and moving your attention toward chasing joy. It's up to you as an individual to reject the idea of this "power save" as a guilty pleasure or low priority. It is a necessity and can provide a much-needed boost for your magic!

As you explored in the first chapter of this book, the magic you're trying to attract is called in by cultivating a vibe. This requires pausing the endless tasks and drudgery and taking some time to simply *feel into* your joy and happiness. You'll manifest better when you're operating from a frequency of mindfulness. And you achieve that by sinking deeply into moments that make you feel connected, present, and whole.

A life devoid of mindful intention has the tendency to tick away on autopilot. In that space it's simply too easy to get lost in your own mental BS and limiting beliefs, making happiness and getting ahead of your reactions more challenging. The solution? Taking moments and even days off to chase your impulses, laze around, play outside, or feed your soul with play and creativity. It's a simple treatment witches use for a pervasive curse, and it has benefits that extend beyond the metaphysical into your overall wellness.

To gain the full benefits of shifting your vibe with a short power save, consider which actions fill you with happy, relaxed feelings, and do that shit more often. This relates to not just the body but the mind as well. The simple break in thought makes meditation feel like a rest, as does sitting on a bench and just watching the ocean. Find your preferred modes of conserving your energy and try to incorporate them into your life on a regular basis.

Last but not least: Never, ever buy into the garbage idea that a break is selfish or something you do when you have "extra time." It should be given the same priority as going to therapy or to the pharmacy to pick up a medication. It should be given the same priority as energetically cleansing yourself or your space. It should be given the same priority as writing up an invoice for your time. Hitting that power-save button is a necessity for functioning, and not something you earn from doing enough.

There is big, beautiful magic in indulging in power-saving mode. So lower your expectations and do less!

A Resting Sigil

Create a sigil and put it out where you will see it while you indulge yourself with rest, as a reminder that what you are doing is an important and intentional part of your wellness. A sigil is a magical symbol charged with your intentions. There are a few different methods of sigil-making. Some would have you take out repeating letters or vowels, but for this sigil, keeping all the letters is fine, as there are four, so they won't get too cluttered.

To craft the sigil, write out the word "REST" on a piece of paper in capital letters, arranging the letters in a way that's pleasing to the eye and feels "right" for you. In my own workings, I tend to arrange them to fit in a simple circle. It may take a few tries to have it turn out the way you want, but it will be worth it. Once you have your final design, make a "good copy" on another piece of paper that you can put on display. Feel free to get creative and use paint, pastels, etc. to bring the design to life. You can even use powdered herbs, tea, essential oils, or moon water to add to your design.

To charge your sigil: There are a few different ways to charge a sigil. You can charge it using energy work or meditation or by focusing on it with an energetic release. You can also charge a sigil under the moonlight, just as you would charge crystals. I personally find that using focused intent and directing energy through the palms works just fine for charging and activating sigils for most work. Take some time to find a method that works best for you.

Create a Safe Space to Be Honest

Happy witches are the ones who dare take the trouble to get cozy with all aspects of the human experience—for better or for worse! This is why witches pursue shadow work, diving into their darkness to find the light. However, this process is easier said than done, especially when you're dealing with traumas and anxieties that feel so overwhelming that you may not even dare speak them aloud. How do you integrate and work on the things that feel so difficult they become taboo in your own consciousness?

The typical avenues for working with these shadows include things like therapy or journaling, but some of your burdens may feel so dark and secretive that you hold on to them in shame rather than speak their truth. In other cases, experience with invasions of privacy or a lack of support can cause hesitation when it comes to unloading these burdens. Regardless of the specifics of *why* you hold these difficult things clutched to your chest, what you need is to give yourself a safe space to be honest as you practice your shadow work.

To be clear, there is nothing wrong with having secrets and dark shadows that you keep only to yourself. Where the problem arises is if these burdens, left undealt with, rot away within your spirit and erode your happiness. Open yourself up to the fact that you are carrying shame that is not yours. Commit to finding your magic in the dark corners of the unpleasant. Take your power back by facing your demons and stripping them of their mystery. When you coax out these shadows, you can heal them—but you need to have a safe space to do that without fear of reprisal or retribution.

The following activity will help you make space to connect with your deepest, darkest shadows by laying them bare in an impermanent way that won't be seen by outside eyes. This is a practice for you and you only, leaving no residue that would leave you open to judgment and reprisal. It is a very personal part of your craft. The hope is that in acknowledging the wounds that linger within, you can take your power back, learning their form and function so that you can move forward toward healing. Of course, I must stress that if you are dealing with heavy trauma, it is imperative to get proper professional help. That being said, rituals like the one that follows can be a good middle step to desensitize yourself from the pain they cause while giving yourself the strength and confidence to go seek help.

You deserve to feel safe. You don't deserve the blame for things that happened to you. And if you made a poor choice in the past, the burden of guilt doesn't have to weigh you down forever. People make mistakes all the time, sometimes catastrophic ones. This is simply a side effect of being alive. You deserve the medicine that comes from taking the lessons, reevaluating, and forgiving yourself. You deserve to be healed and be happy. You are worthy of wonderful feelings and great things, full stop!

A Salt Writing Activity

As you learned previously, this activity will guide you as you process or "get out" some of your deepest secrets and traumas, without leaving traces that can be found by others. This is a completely safe space for you and you alone to work with your darkest issues.

Materials

- Cleansing tools of your choice
- A large shallow bowl or dish
- Finely ground salt (enough to fill bowl)
- 1–2 tablespoons finely crushed dried chamomile

Instructions

1. Cleanse your materials and yourself. Make sure to affirm to yourself that you are safe and protected, making a special commitment to check in emotionally and abort the activity should it get too uncomfortable for you. Your mental health and comfort are always of the highest priority.

2. Fill your bowl with the salt and the calming chamomile.

3. Take the index finger of your right hand and make swirls in the bowl, mixing the salt and the herbs as you go.

4. Using the index finger of your dominant hand, begin writing in the salt. You can write out your secrets, the things you long to hear to heal, or just simply tell your story. This is for whatever feels right and best for you!

5. Make sure to take deep breaths in through your nose and out through your mouth and remain in a state of focused, present awareness throughout this process. The point is to connect with these things, letting them move both through and out of you so that you can feel lighter and unburdened afterward.

Fall in Love with Surrender

Powerful witchcraft is often a marriage between mundane action and total surrender. Although it can feel counterintuitive to let go when you are trying to achieve or call in something, it is an imperative part of the process, especially if you want to be happy while you are trying to manifest. There is an element of trust that's required, a belief that things will work in the ways they need to in order for your best good, even if you can't quite make out *how* in the moment.

Clinging is no way to pursue happy. In order to let the full expansion of joy in, you must release expectations and surrender to the unique timing of your life. Of course, it's far easier in hindsight to recognize that losing things you wanted can be a blessing or to see how turns in the road directed you toward great things. In the moment it can just feel frustrating and confusing AF.

Relax and breathe!

You can (and should!) try to shift your life in the direction you want with the tools at your disposal. You can work for it, build the foundations, and use your witchy practices as a boost to get things done. But at the end of the day, sometimes things just don't go the way you want, or they take longer to work out than you would prefer. For better or for worse, at a certain point you need to let go, if only just to give yourself some peace and reprieve from holding on too tight. You need to learn to fall in love with the exhilarating rush of surrender. Of letting go.

The more you cling to things, the less likely you are to see the brilliant opportunities that swirl all around you. What a fortunate thing it can be to be delivered from the things you thought you once wanted! Although trusting the timing of your life can cause you to feel resistance, as if you're flirting with giving up, if anything, it's the opposite. You can surrender to the timing of your life while simultaneously holding space for your goals and aspirations. It just requires a little flexibility, patience, openness, and a willingness to persist in the belief that good things are coming. It's really about not giving in to the narrow vibe of tunnel vision.

So if you want to be happier, let loose the reins a little bit. Surrender to the timing of your life and be comfortable with not always being able to direct or micromanage the outcome. Although it may not be easy, the most rewarding things rarely are. If you base your happiness on things going as planned, you will find yourself up against a wall over and over. Let it go, let it flow, and remain in the frequency of gratitude and joy. This is where the magic happens!

A Ritual to Surrender to the Timing of Your Life

This is a ritual to be performed in those times when things are not happening for you at the pace you had hoped. It is simple and requires no tools except your own breath and discipline in releasing the need to have things go the way you planned. This ritual is best done when there is windy weather; however, even a slight breeze will do.

1. Stand outside and place your feet shoulder-width apart. Take some deep, cleansing breaths in through your nose and out through your mouth to ground and center yourself.

2. Place one hand on your chest and the other on your belly (just under your rib cage). Inhale deeply through your nose, imagining that in doing so you are stabilizing any anxiety or stress.

3. As you exhale, picture all the pent-up frustration leaving your body through your breath.

4. Once you feel adequately grounded, raise your arms into the air and chant, "I relinquish control and surrender to the timing of my life." Repeat this for as long as you need, until you begin to feel lighter, allowing the feeling of trust to wash over you. As you do this, you may feel the desire to sway and move in the breeze. This is the flow you are seeking, so feel free to lean into it! This is a sacred dance of connection, of feeling the rush of the wind on your body. The essence of surrender is being able to vibe in the not knowing, supported by trusting the Universe and the unique timing of how things unfold, even if they don't match up with your best laid plans.

Take Time to Honor Balance

Life is full of ups and downs, and as cheesy as it sounds, the old platitudes are correct: It's how you respond to them that can make or break you. This isn't to say that you're failing in some way if you let the hard times knock you over—just the opposite, in fact! Perhaps the most important part of this roller coaster is to really experience whatever it is where you're at, while still holding space for the fact that it *will* change. This is the beauty and chaos of balance.

A fundamental part of being able to shift into a happier state is to really understand that your emotions and your circumstances are transitory. Every situation eventually turns into some other situation, and the emotions that can feel crippling today *will* gradually shift into something more pleasant. Having a solid grasp of this concept of balance can be a lifesaver in troubled times. It can act as your lighthouse in those moments when it can feel as if you're lost in the dark—seeing troubled times as a sacred doorway that can lead to new growth.

Here's the reality: Sometimes things will just suck, and sometimes things will be great. These are opposing ends of the wheel of fortune that is always turning, as everyone hangs on for dear life and does their best to get their bearings. The ups and downs and everything in between make up the fabric of existence. In this eternal balance, every high is valid. Every low is valid. And all of it is *necessary*.

Balance is a constant, a beautiful and fundamental force that can both refresh and deplete you, depending on where you find yourself. This might be a tough pill to swallow, but fortunately, you can game the system when it comes to mindset. Instead of fighting the ebbs and flows, ultimately feeling worse for it, you can lean into the joy of the good times and let the memory of them keep you warm in the times when worries and doubts and dramas have you caught up in the downswing.

Although it's become more fashionable to dismiss cultivating a more positive outlook as being "toxic," the truth is that your brain naturally tends to dwell a little longer on negative things. Obviously, throwing "Just think positive!" at any problem is kinda useless advice that doesn't factor in the nuances of reality and personal circumstance, but that doesn't take the power away from positive thinking as an incredibly beneficial tool in your witchcraft reservoir. You would be wise to cultivate a mindset that recognizes the balance of the human experience—that there are good times and bad—and to train your awareness to vibe in the good times for just a little longer. People don't seem to have an issue with knowing that the good times will eventually end, but for some reason it's a struggle to truly buy into the fact that the tides can shift in your favor when things aren't going well. And the trouble is that if you don't *believe* this is true, then you have the potential to miss it when it happens. You essentially become comfortable in misery rather than allowing the wheel of fortune to take you on its crazy ride, allowing yourself to be present for both the highs and the lows.

In order to fully enjoy life in all of its moody seasons, you must take the time to honor and hold space for all points of the wheel on this roller-coaster ride. Sometimes your spirit is alight with joy and hope, and sometimes you have just dimming embers to keep you warm. This is okay and a normal, fundamental part of the human experience that unites everyone across the board.

A Sensory Bottle Meditation

The following can make meditation a little more fun. This practice is especially good for those who struggle with meditation or keeping focus while doing this sort of work (neurodivergent witches, unite!).

Materials

- Cleansing tools of your choice
- A small, clear plastic bottle with a lid
- Water (enough to fill half of bottle)
- 5–6 drops food coloring (green and blue are recommended for the calming and healing correspondences, but feel free to experiment!)
- Baby oil or olive oil (enough to fill up the remaining half of bottle)*
- Glue

*Olive oil will give the mixture a yellowish hue, while baby oil is clear. It's up to you which to use; baby oil is a bit more expensive but a good option if you want the mixture to be more aesthetically pleasing.

Instructions

1. Cleanse your space and your materials and use your magical energy to set your intention to infuse this meditation bottle with calm, grounded, and healing energy.

2. Take the bottle and fill halfway with water.

3. Add 4 drops of green food coloring and 1–2 drops of blue food coloring, then put the cap on and shake to mix.

4. Open up the bottle and fill the rest of the way with baby oil or olive oil.

5. Place glue on the inside of the bottle cap to keep it sealed shut. You do *not* want anyone drinking or spilling this!

6. Shake wildly and watch the bubbles swirl and mix with the colored water.

7. Sit in a safe, comfortable position, at a time and place where you're probably not going to be interrupted.

8. Take 3–6 deep cleansing breaths in through your nose and out through your mouth to ground yourself and your energy.

9. Now think about your life, the good times and the bad. As you do this, shake your bottle vigorously and roll it around in your hands.

10. Watch how the mixture bubbles and swirls, and as you tip it over and roll it in your hands, meditate on the transient nature of the human experience. If it's helpful, tell yourself affirmations that tie to this lesson, such as "All things eventually move and shift" and "Life is a beautiful mixing of highs and lows."

11. If your oil and water start separating again, keep shaking. The point is to keep your hands busy and your eyes focused on the swirling bubbles, as this can be a helpful way to stay in the moment.

Give Names to Your Ghosts

It can be all too tempting to gloss over the hard bits in your quest to become happier. Naturally, the scars you carry and the traumas you've been through can be chilling reminders of the darker aspects of life, and to sit with them can leave you feeling anything but joy. Everyone carries ghosts; some linger behind you, just outside your perception, while others hang off of you, their presence impossible to ignore. In all of these cases, what's needed is to face them head-on, setting them free so they can haunt you no longer.

These ghosts may be events, circumstances, or other shadows that played a role in the emergence of who you are as a person. They can be things that can be hard to define, yet you feel them weighing you down, making moving with joy seem like an incredibly hard task.

But hard doesn't mean impossible!

A large part of the witch's journey through magic is learning to work with these shadows. Although it can be heavy to give them a seat at the table and ask them what they seek from you, it is heavier still to shut the door on them, pretending that in not giving them an audience you are shutting them out completely. Witches know better! It is not your attention that gives these ghosts life, but the withholding of it that drives them to remain stuck to you, clamoring to be heard, to be integrated, and to be released.

It's time to take your power back.

As challenging as it may sound, you must give form to the things that haunt you. You must sit with your ghosts, and learn from them, before they sabotage you in all the little ways that leave you feeling halted and stuck. Your demons don't need to be outrun; they need to be kindly asked, "What purpose do you serve?" Compassion and love extended to these ghosts is a simple medicine that can allow you to move forward in a lighter way with ease.

The ability to transform and transmute pain into power is one of the hallmarks of witchcraft. This is but one way to reclaim your happiness, allowing the dark shadows that hang around the corners of your awareness to be cleansed and released through the light of your kindness and understanding. And once addressed, your ghosts can actually become some of your greatest allies! They can give you some insight into the things in your life that need healing or forgiveness or to just be thanked and sent off on their merry way.

It's time to stretch those witchy muscles and liberate yourself from hiding from the hard things. To allow yourself to be brave and explore these dark caverns of your shadows. In doing so, you can cut ties with their heaviness and move forward in a way that is freer and more balanced.

A Spell for Cutting Ties with Your Ghosts

The following spell will help you cut ties with your own ghosts, thanking them for the protective purpose they served while allowing them to be turned into something lighter and more beneficial for your best interests.

Materials

- Cleansing tools of your choice
- A small black bowl or small cauldron
- Water (enough to fill bowl or cauldron)
- A black candle

Instructions

1. Begin by cleansing yourself and your materials with the method of your choice. Do some grounding and centering, or cast a protective circle if this works well for you.

2. Fill your black bowl or cauldron with the water and light the black candle. Affirm which ghosts you are giving an audience to (perhaps it is a specific traumatic event or a situation where you regret your part, or something more general that needs releasing) as you light your candle.

3. Gaze into the water illuminated by the candlelight. Meditate on these wounds, why they haunt you, and how it might feel to release all the baggage attached to it. As you do this, allow your mind to explore the issue, and truly sit with the discomfort. Eventually, you may begin to feel lighter, or make mental connections on the reasons this was so impactful or the things you can learn from them.

4. Once ready, thank these ghosts for their audience, and send them on their way by blowing out your candle.

5. Pour the water outside, away from your house and near a back door, to be carried away.

CHAPTER 5

Be Connected

Humans are social creatures; we need the companionship and camaraderie of others to help us lead happy, successful lives. Even the most introverted, solitary witches can glean joy from relationships and connections that help them feel "seen" and understood. There is a special kind of magic that comes from your relationships with others, one that can be boosted by having a good relationship with *yourself*. In many cases, interpersonal stressors are amplified by not facing your own inner wounds, causing you to imprint your insecurities and will onto other people. And you may feel you need to play by rules or repress certain parts of yourself in the name of acceptance, when the truth is that in showing up in your authenticity, you are able to attract more meaningful relationships with those who would accept you fully.

In this chapter, you will use the craft to get to know yourself and love yourself better, and give yourself what you need, so you can go forth and connect with the people around you in beneficial ways. You will use spellcasting, rituals, and more to spread love and kindness to others as a way to embody the magic you seek for yourself. Through witchcraft, you will find joy through these purposeful connections, and joy through the lessons you get from working through social and intrapersonal challenges.

Romance Yourself

Imagine being in a long-term relationship where your needs are constantly put on the back burner. Imagine this relationship being a place for put-downs, disparaging talk about your character, and emotional bullying. I think it would be safe to say that such a relationship would need some serious work or a shift in dynamics!

Now imagine that this is a relationship between you and yourself.

Self-love is truly not all that different from romantic love: It doesn't happen overnight, and it takes a lot of work, strength, grace, and patience. A healthy relationship with yourself is not something that is built and left to stand. Instead, it is like any other relationship—it needs to be nurtured and fed as it evolves and changes over time. Although many people tend to think of self-love as this prize that's won at the completion of a healing journey, this way of thinking does a massive disservice to the work that's *actually* required. It is an ongoing process that's much like a video game with various levels and "final bosses" but no big "end." You have to step up in order to send yourself and the Universe the message that you are committed to your growth. Like romantic love, it's a roller coaster of feels that has the potential for a whole lot of happiness!

Although self-love can feel like a million miles away when starting from a place of low self-esteem, it all begins with a single step. Whether it's a simple promise of self-acceptance or some extra acts of tenderness toward yourself, all the seemingly small steps along the road make massive waves of change that wash over your life experience. Try treating yourself as a lover, curiously probing the depths of your spirit in an open and accepting way. It starts with gentleness and tenderness—treat yourself kindly and the rest will naturally fall in line! When focusing on self-acceptance, you will undoubtedly see what others do: that you are a wonderful human being having a chaotic human experience, just like every other person on this planet.

Be open to allowing yourself to fall in love with who you are. Just as you can recognize that perfection doesn't exist in romantic relationships, allow *yourself* also to be absolved of needing to be perfect in order to be lovable. You are worthy as you are, full stop. You always have been! It's time to start treating yourself like it, because at the end of the day, inside that powerful little skull of yours, it's only you and yourself—and you want that to be a safe place to be!

Now, depending on your upbringing and/or the social expectations you grew up with, you may have been raised to view confidence as a selfish thing. Many women especially can feel this pressure to never focus on themselves. This can make the hill toward self-love feel like even *more* of a climb straight off the jump. However, the pursuit of happiness is just as much (if not more so) about unlearning as it is about learning. It involves peeling back the dead weight of what only drags you down in the pursuit of light, breezy joy. Again, it is a journey! Start taking steps toward self-love now, and you'll be surprised at where you end up.

A Mirror Activity for Self-Love and Acceptance

The mirror has been one of the most revolutionary tools I found in my own practice for confidence and self-love, and the following activity is designed to help you build your self-love. For this ritual you will simply need a mirror. Full-length is best; however, I personally do this one a lot prior to bath rituals in my ordinary bathroom mirror.

1. Light some candles and put on some mood music. Have enough light available that you can see yourself clearly in the mirror.

2. Breathe deeply in through your nose and out through your mouth, and do any grounding and centering to get into a good magical mindset.

3. Gaze at your reflection, into your own eyes, and speak aloud some affirmations that are unique to you. As you do so, you may find that you feel uncomfortable or silly—move past it. Look at your physical form. Look at the things you love, and the things that make you feel insecure.

4. Continue to gaze at your reflection and move through the complex emotions that come up when you do. Do not resist these feelings; simply let them pass. Sit with them until the discomfort eases. Counter any negative self-talk with statements of love. Tell yourself the things you long to hear!

5. Commit to loving the witch staring back at you in all their perfectly imperfect glory!

6. Blow out the candles, and as you do, make "wishes" for yourself (for peace, clarity, confidence, etc.).

Clean Up Your Trash Talk

Because we are social creatures, it can be really challenging for us humans to pass up on the chance for some hot, juicy gossip. It's a shadow side of our nature to find entertainment in the trials and misadventures of others. And it's not necessarily that we delight in it, but perhaps we just feel vindicated by it—a sign that others are going through the same petty miseries that we are!

That being said, happiness thrives in the absence of comparison, gossiping, and talking negatively (a.k.a. shit-talking) in all forms. True joy multiplies when *everyone* thrives. The boost that is obtained from talking trash is never a solid foundation for anything positive, and instead makes a statement about who you are and how you feel inside in that moment. Most people have the experience at some point in life of discovering when they've been the topic of conversation; it never feels good. This is important to remember when you feel the desire to engage in spilling the tea. Are you willing to be the source of hurt and negative feelings in another person?

Those are some bad vibes, witch!

Witches know that words are spells, and you need to be careful of what you are speaking into existence. You must be aware of what you are giving life to with your words and your energy—not just for yourself but for others too. It's like the old saying that if you can't say something nice, then don't say anything at all. To glean entertainment from another person's struggles or hardships is not the vibe for cultivating true happiness or joy. At best it would be like junk food for your soul: tasty in the moment, but, at the end of the day, still unhealthy.

On the other hand, it feels good to be happy for people, to root for them and encourage their successes. You can feel it in your heart space when you well up with pride on behalf of someone you love, even if you are rooting for them from afar. This compassionate talk gives a more lasting substance and raises your own energy, while ragging on folks only serves to lower your vibration so that you can feel either superior or less alone in your own misfortunes.

Happiness is fertilized by love—not just love for the self but love for those around you. So if you want to be happier and improve your relationships, watch the way you talk very closely, and cut yourself off from idle gossip and drama. Cast loving spells with your words. At the end of the day, everyone is in this human experience together, and you can make it lighter and better for yourself if you treat others with dignity and respect rather than poisoning your own vibe with negativity and pettiness.

A Sweetening Spell to Curb Negative Talk and Gossip

The following is a spell to sweeten your tongue so that you use it in ways that uplift, heal, and encourage, rather than put down others for the sake of a cheap conversation.

Materials

- An apple
- 1 teaspoon honey

Instructions

1. Hold the apple between your palms. Take a few deep breaths in through your nose and out through your mouth and feel the energy swirling in your body.

2. Raise and direct this energy to go through your palms into the apple. As you do this, think about the kind of friend and person you want to be—someone who is supportive and uplifting, who is nourished by the same kind of loving energy that you put out.

3. Put the honey on the tip of a spoon. Dip your forefinger in the honey, then dab it on your top and bottom lip. State aloud your intention to use your voice in loving, supportive defense of others, and your intention to reject the urge to use your sacred breath to gossip or talk badly of others.

4. While the honey is still on your lips, begin eating the apple. When finished, compost or bury the core outside.

5. After you perform this spell, use your voice to tell someone you care about just how much you support and appreciate them.

Call In Self-Trust

Although self-love has become the poster child for confidence and freedom from your own neuroses (and it is important!), self-trust is really the backbone that allows you to act from your power. It is what all of your magic is built on.

What exactly is self-trust? Well, it comes down to knowing your needs and being fully accepting of who you are. This allows you to take care of yourself in a respectful and responsible manner, recognizing that you can handle what life throws at you. With a solid foundation of self-trust, you can rely on yourself to make decisions and forward movements that work toward your own best interests. It is truly one of the most foundational principles to lead a happier life. Often overlooked or taken for granted, working on healing your relationship with yourself and calling in self-trust is one of the most transformative ways to empower yourself in your everyday life. You'll be a happier, stronger witch for it.

It's a pretty big deal!

So how do you start the tricky work of learning to trust yourself? First and foremost you need to be open and accepting of who you are and make the commitment to break free of your own limitations. People tend to suffer far too much based on ideas that are not rooted in reality. You may think you aren't good enough, that you aren't worthy, and all too often believe things about yourself that are not necessarily true. Self-trust is built on self-acceptance: knowing who you are, from the good to the bad and, yes, the ugly. Self-trust is not an exercise in "fake it till you make it"; instead, it is a deep uncovering of what lies within and a commitment to using this information in order to step up to your life in a more confident and secure manner.

Part of this task is being able to connect with your inner guidance and higher selves, doing things that feel right and good. Your happiness takes the hit when you move against your heart, spirit, and better judgments. This is why so many poor decisions come from high-pressure situations that induce emotions such as lack and fear. Although you may *feel* like you are doing yourself a service in the moment, you're often left regretting not trusting your heart and instincts. This is what inspires the sentiments that magic lies on the other side of fear. Self-trust can act as the bridge, propelling you into a full life of thriving!

One thing that's important to note when talking about self-trust: You are not required to be "correct" in order to trust your inner guidance. People are wrong all the time, so being "right" is not the correct metric when it comes to calling in self-trust. The difference is that when you move from a place of self-trust, you can be confident that you are making the best decisions you can, given the information you have at the time. This lessens regret and promotes resilience. Sometimes you may get it wrong, and it just is what it is. But when you move in self-trust, you can always commend yourself for moving in alignment with your heart and your spirit.

Call in self-trust, and allow happiness to bloom in its wake!

A Self-Trust Spell

The following spell is designed to deepen the connection to the self and call in self-trust, including letting go of the fears and anxieties that come with worrying that you are going to make the wrong moves.

Materials

- Cleansing tools of your choice
- A yellow or white candle
- A lighter
- A mirror

Instructions

1. Begin by cleansing and grounding yourself, your space, and your materials however you choose.

2. Sit and reflect on your unique relationship with self-trust.

3. When ready, light your candle and hold it in your dominant hand. Hold it up to the mirror and say, "May the light of this flame act as a beacon of trust—trust in myself and trust in my power. I am capable of all things that are meant for me, and I am open and receptive to the voice of wisdom that lies within me."

4. Still holding your candle, imagine a small seed of light that starts in your forehead, in the third eye area, and visualize it slowly growing and expanding throughout your body, flowing through your arm and into the candle.

5. Place your other hand on the mirror and imagine that that same light energy is flowing both toward and from yourself as you gaze into your own eyes in the mirror.

6. Continuing to breathe, imagine what it would feel like to have a solid foundation of self-trust. Visualize the light inside you becoming a conduit for the confident, unwavering energy that comes with perfect self-trust.

7. When you feel it, allow yourself to feel gratitude. Gratitude for who you are, who you have been, and who you're becoming.

8. Blow out your candle in the direction of your reflection. Take three deep breaths and ground your energy again. Pay close attention to your inner guidance as you move forward after completing this spell.

Honor Your Separateness

"It takes all types to make a world," or so the saying goes—a very polite way of saying that we're all so bizarre in our own special ways that it would be impossible for us to agree on everything! This can be the source of a lot of unnecessary stress in the relationship domain—all too often, we exert our precious energy trying to get people to see things our way or, even worse, we try to control how other people will receive us. This is a huge hole in our "energetic bucket" (our source of energy that we draw from and refill), and it's only in honoring separateness that real peace can be found, regardless of what other people are doing. This is a magical act of energetic protection, a metaphorical way to cast a circle around ourselves so that we will be able to happily thrive, independent of what others are doing.

Human existence and societies are very interpersonal. Your close relationships can feel like a merging of spirits and energies, which can be a beautiful source of intimacy. However, the shadow side of this is that you can slip into clinging and controlling your loved ones by not honoring the fact that you are distinctly separate from them. This means that you may disagree with them on big things, they may make choices that upset or confuse you, or they may judge and misinterpret you personally. All of these are situations where you can lapse into the bad habit of trying to control what they do or think, which is ultimately a recipe for nothing but frustration.

True happiness can be conjured when you banish this BS!

In order to be happy, you need to release the desire to control other people—how they think, how they see you, and how they interpret the world around them. And although you may feel resistance at the suggestion that this comes from a place of control, it certainly does. Control shows itself in many ways. Every time you feel the need to prove others wrong or overexplain your position in order to be considered "right" or "valid" by others, what you're doing is effectively trying to force them into aligning with your perspective. And in doing so, you are handing your power away. You are communicating that the other person's stance has some power over your well-being or happiness. For a sovereign witch, this is simply not the case. You must cultivate your own happiness and comfort independently of what anyone else is doing or thinking.

This desire to have people be on the same side as you, to have them understand you, or to influence them to come over to your side will be a consistent source of misery if you let it. Everyone is different, and just as your viewpoints and opinions have been shaped by your unique circumstances, so have others'. This can be a beautiful thing. In allowing everyone to be different, to be separate, to be unique, you open yourself up to new and novel experiences. There is the potential for you to gather, to learn from others, and to inspire others.

Are there people out there with hateful opinions and ideas? Yes. Are there times when you are misinterpreted and it can cause very real problems for you? Also yes. But the thing is, these situations are likely to happen whether you attempt to control them or not. All you can do is your best to educate others or find common ground in an attempt to forge some understanding. At the end of the day, people are going to do and think what they choose, and all your best efforts might just be akin to banging your head against the wall.

Reclaim your power and cast some boundaries, witch!

You are separate, as is everyone around you. Just as you would like your perspectives and uniqueness to be recognized, you need to extend that grace to others. Allow for the special differences of all, making space for all the good and not-so-good that comes with it.

A Separation Meditation

Do this meditation whenever you have to deal with large groups of people, or after you find yourself in situations where you've struggled to let other people be separate from you.

1. Light some incense, grab some crystals, and sit in a comfortable, relaxed position somewhere you are unlikely to be disturbed.

2. Begin deep breathing in through your nose and out through your mouth to get yourself in a calm and magical zone.

3. Start thinking of all the unique qualities that make up the person that you are.

4. Visualize your energy flowing through your body, seeping out of your pores, and creating an aura that is around your person. Visualize its color, its shape, and its form. Is it thick? Is it opaque? Imagine this aura as a protective bubble that keeps your energy safe and close to your physical body.

5. Now think about other people and how they, too, have these bubbles, and how these bubbles are unique to them. Their colors may be different, their form may stray in appearance from yours. Allow your mind to imagine how your interactions with others can shift these auras and your energy in various ways.

6. As you meditate, really focus on the integrity of your own bubble. How are you spending your interpersonal energy? Is your energetic field a solid energetic barrier for you, or is it leaking and reaching all over the place?

7. As you continue to breathe, think about how wonderful it is that we are all autonomous and separate unique beings.

Be Soft but Not to Be Messed With

Misunderstandings, pushed boundaries, and betrayals—these are just but a few of the ways that interpersonal relationships can impede happiness. That being said, there is even more good to be had from your social connections. You cannot allow the fear of conflict or hurt to interfere with how you approach relationships with other people. What you do need to do is have a solid foundation of what you will and will not accept, making sure that you are gentle, flexible, and balanced in how you respond to others, even in the face of drama and chaos.

The natural world is an endless source of inspiration for the witch. There is a lot that can be learned from the natural forces, the cosmos, and the elements. Everything in the world offers inspiration and guidance for magical work. Take water, for instance. Water can be fluid and flexible, yet it also has the capacity to be solid and unyielding. You can learn a thing or two about the importance of this balance. This lesson can be especially useful in your connections with other people.

Like water, you can be soft but not to be messed with. This is the essence of bringing love and boundaries into your relationships!

Your connections with others can be a beautiful source of joy and pleasure. However, these connections can sometimes drain and deplete you if you allow the wrong people in or if you set the precedent of letting other people push your boundaries and impose their BS on you. Relationships are tricky, and although meme culture has reduced the complexities of these relationships down to just dismissing others as toxic if they push you, the truth is that everyone is human. Everyone is doing their best, and sometimes people mess up because of whatever they are going through—not necessarily because they are ill-intentioned. This is why boundaries are important in all relationships. Whether it be with your family, your partner, or even your acquaintances, boundaries are imperative for protecting yourself and your wellness when coping with other people.

To be soft is to be fluid and flexible, which means that you should also be compassionate, even in the face of adversity with others. Your boundaries do not need to be iron gates that hold people out forever. In fact, you should normalize being open to the fact that other people are as flawed as you are. Everyone is moving through this tumultuous human experience, and *everyone* tends to mess up from time to time. You may be tempted to cut people off and label them as bad for you—or think that's what you "should" do because it's what other people say is "right"—when the truth is rarely so black and white. Sometimes it may be appropriate to make allowances, provided you are ensuring that your happiness and well-being are taken into consideration.

You are not meant to have a one-size-fits-all response to life. In an ever-changing world, with an ever-changing life filled with people trying their best, it is important to adapt, to flow, and to respond in a way that's measured and resilient. You can be happier in general if you choose ease and flow over rigid ideas of how you think you "should" respond to any given situation. Your happiness will grow from a balance of being soft yet firm.

A Boundaries Ward

Wards are a type of defensive magic that are meant to protect your spaces from spiritual, energetic, and mundane intrusions. Aloe vera can serve as a great ward. It is a plant that manages to be both spiky and healing—it has perfect "be soft but not to be fucked with" energy! Aloe plants are succulents and can do pretty well indoors in most areas, provided they are cared for properly (this depends on a lot of factors, including available light, humidity in the air, etc.).

In order to use an aloe plant as a ward for boundaries, pluck and curl one of your hairs around the base of the plant or, if repotting, around the roots. Ask the plant to be your ward against interpersonal issues, but also state your commitment to have your boundaries be fair and measured.

To boost your ward, place an Apache tear crystal (for forgiveness) and a Temperance tarot card near your plant. As you care for your plant, keep in mind its protective purpose, and refresh its link to you and your energy when necessary by using energy work and/or adding another hair.

Give Love with Abandon

When imagining the things that you need in order to be happy, it's easy to compile quite the list. Is it success? Things? Changing some fundamental aspect of yourself or your appearance? In a world where consumption is a pastime, you can slip into the bad habit of spending to fill the hole to get to that happy state, seeing your joy as being on the other side of the next thing you can change, do, or purchase.

What you *really* need is love...and that shit's *free*!

Love is an incredible dimension of the human experience. It frightens and inspires, is the topic of countless songs and poems, and motivates people to do great and sometimes terrible things. Love is a fundamental need, which is probably why it appears as a central tenet in most world religions, and why it's frequently the main takeaway from profound meditative and psychedelic experiences. "It's all love, man." As cheesy as it may sound, this *is* the answer. This is the top of the emotional mountain—the peak, the pinnacle!

And it's a beautiful thing. Not just the romantic form, but love in *all* its forms. When you give love freely, you open yourself up to more loving feelings in general. Your happiness and joy multiply, as love is one of the most powerful vibrations that you can lean into. Think of an occasion where you felt love—the effect that it had on your body and your emotional state, how it affected your perception of time, and your overall mindset toward the world. When you lean into love, you are moving into a frequency that is positively transcendent, and the longer you vibe in that space, the better the return for your health and happiness.

That being said, love can be scary. It can be very vulnerable to express love, especially if you grew up in circumstances where visible love was in short supply or experienced a heartbreak that still weighs on you. Part of healing this wound is to untangle your complex feelings toward love, including how you express it, how it feels for you, and which shadows may be getting in the way of you showing up to your life in a more loving way. It should be a goal to give love with as much reckless abandon as you can muster. Is it vulnerable to do this? Yes. But witches are not the types to shy away from the challenging stuff! They understand that shadow work like this is just as important as, if not more important than, any other part of their magical practices.

You don't need to be a "love and light" kind of witch to recognize the immense healing power of love—both in the giving and the receiving of it. Although it can be hard to lead with love in a world that can feel chaotic and unjust, to do so is a powerful way to push back against the disconnection and chaos that tend to be characteristic of modern-day life. To move with love is a reclamation of power. It's choosing to show up in a way that's open, soft, and vulnerable. So be big with your love. Love is the vibe, and the more love you give, the more you (and those around you) thrive!

A Blessing Jar for Expressing Love

This is a spell that can be done in order to send love and blessings to people from a distance. You could use this if you are a business owner to bless your buyers, or you could even use it to bless a particular group that you have issues with, as a way to fight drama with love and positivity. This is by far my favorite love spell, as it allows you to send love and positive energy to multiple people, and while performing the spell, you get a loving boost as well.

Materials

- Cleansing tools of your choice
- A red candle
- Small strips of paper (as many as you have names to add to your jar)
- A pen
- A small jar
- Salt*
- Ground cinnamon*
- Dried jasmine buds*
- Dried rose petals*

*You will want enough to create equal layers of these ingredients in the jar.

Instructions

1. Begin by cleansing yourself and your materials and opening up a magical space.

2. Light your candle and meditate on the people you are wanting to send love and blessings to and why. Allow yourself to feel the emotions that come up when you think of your intent. For example, if you are doing a blessing jar to send love to people who have supported you, allow yourself to lean into those feelings of love and gratitude.

3. On your strips of paper, write down the names of the people you are wanting to send your love to. Roll the strips up into little paper cylinders.

4. Add the ingredients to your jar in the following order: salt, cinnamon, your rolled-up papers, jasmine buds, and rose petals.

5. Hold your jar between your palms, take some deep breaths, and raise your energy from your heart space, through your body, up through your arms and into the jar. The goal is to infuse your jar with loving, positive emotion.

6. Keep your jar somewhere it will be seen regularly for at least one week. Feel free to shake the jar when you want to give an extra loving boost!

7. If you have a firepit, you can burn the contents of the jar in a little ceremony following the week as an added step.

Take the Time to Truly See People

It's become a cliché at this point how incredibly connected we are globally, yet how disconnected we can feel at the same time. Although this is certainly not true for everybody, there are many people who feel isolated and alone in the hectic soup of modern life. This is a strange time in human history where we can have access to people from all over the world literally in the palms of our hands (through our devices), yet many of us can go through days or even weeks without getting so much as a smile from other humans on the street. It's like there is a hidden cloak of invisibility that a lot of us wear when out in the real world. We've strayed far from our roots of communal living, of supporting and connecting with one another in the ways that helped our species to thrive for countless years.

A large part of the witch's path is to *be* the magic you want to see in the world. To step up and break ties with the norms that don't serve you in a way that inspires others to break theirs. Witches heal, and this disconnection that is felt in society needs healing in a big way. This means that you must not underestimate the value of your interactions, as mundane as they may seem! This can help you to be happier as an individual as well, as the spark of connection (even with a stranger) can be a wonderful source of light and joy.

The easiest way to break through this armor of disconnection is to give people the simple gift of your time and attention. Listen to them intently, call them by their name, and look them in their eyes. Even something as small and simple as chatting up a cashier or stranger on the street can make a big difference.

These are simple and small actions that can ripple through the collective, helping to heal the whole. Find the joy of connecting with another soul, even if it's just in the mundane. When interacting with people, whether loved ones or strangers, cultivate an energy that is a welcoming space for them: Make eye contact and allow them to feel seen. These are the seeds to propagating connection!

Can you recall times in your life when you were made to feel seen by a stranger? These are likely such memorable experiences because of their impact—even the smallest gestures and tiniest displays of humanity can be so nourishing, especially when the world can feel simultaneously lonely and overpopulated.

Happiness thrives in community, fed by love, respect, and kindness. These are all values that you can choose to embody as you move through the world, setting a precedent for others to do the same. So take the time to truly *see* people. Not only will this be a source of happiness for them, but it will also undoubtedly uplift you in return!

A Human Connection Sachet

Sachets are little bags of magic that you can carry in your bag, pocket, etc. This one uses elements of calm, love, and friendship in order to radiate the kind of energy that shows people that you are safe and open to truly seeing them.

Materials

- Cleansing tools of your choice
- A small drawstring bag

- A favorite perfume or scented spray
- A pinch dried jasmine buds
- A pinch dried rose petals
- A pinch dried thyme
- A pinch bee pollen
- A black moonstone

Instructions

1. Begin by cleansing yourself and your items and opening up a sacred space.

2. Take your bag and spritz your perfume or scent inside of it.

3. Add herbs to your sachet.

4. Hold your moonstone crystal and raise your energy to infuse it with loving, open energy that will act as a beacon for others. Add it to your bag.

5. Hold your assembled bag in both hands and chant or state your intention to "have eyes to see, the will to connect, and the light to share with others." Raise your energy up through your body and into your palms to flow into your sachet.

6. Carry your sachet on you when you go out, and match the magic of it with the mundane act of being kind to people. Look them in the eyes, pause to hear what they have to say, and share your genuine smiles with them. Reap the rewards of showing up to the world in this way!

Give Appreciation

We often think about happiness as something we obtain when we *receive* things. Certainly when we get the things we want, when we are shown love, and when we find success or accomplish something, those are times when we can get a jolt of satisfaction that can make us feel really amazing. However, this is only part of the story. As most of us can attest, we can also invoke incredible happiness when *we* are the ones in the giving seat. As witches, cultivating our energy to be kind, loving, and appreciative can bring huge returns when it comes to our own happiness and well-being. Doing so helps us raise our vibration to a place that is expansive and open for joy.

There is a deep and powerful well of joy that you can tap in to when you put your energy toward helping others, cheering for their successes, and going out of your way to show gratitude and appreciation for them.

It's a fundamental human desire to feel valued, important, and validated. Most people want to feel "seen" and understood, and when somebody out there takes the time to show appreciation for the things you say, do, or create, it is a very special gift that is precious beyond words. Now, obviously, as a writer, I can say there's a great source of happiness when somebody shares with me the positive impact my words have had on them; however, I have also made a habit of showing appreciation to others (even strangers, when their creations and work have touched me) as a way to spread little seeds of happiness that I *also* get to benefit from!

This is a beautiful example of embodying the magic you wish to see in the world. It just feels good to uplift others. Research shows that being kind and positive toward your fellow folks helps you in return, so allowing yourself to freely gush over other people and the impacts they've made on you is a worthwhile investment of your time and energy. Think of the last time you expressed sincere appreciation toward a friend or a stranger: This is anything but a selfless act! It's the kind of pure contagious positivity that helps make the world better. It makes you feel good, the person you're appreciating will feel great, and then they will likely pass it forward with their action—a wonderful example of how joy and positivity have the potential to truly ripple through the collective. There are no small acts of love and appreciation; they are all seeds that grow into more love and kindness in the world.

So tell authors you love their books, tell artists you love their art, tell strangers you love their hair—hell, you can squawk appreciation at the crows! There's enough division and drama in the world, so simple acts like this are what's needed in order for you to thrive in a way that conjures up big joy. Be appreciative.

Appreciation Activities for Showing Your Love

The following is a list of appreciation activities that you can use to spread your love.

- Make handwritten cards to show your appreciation. These can be dressed up with your own art or poetry, as well as with dried herbs or flowers.

- Make an appreciation jar—a loving herb jar such as the one suggested in this book. Add a small piece of paper every time you give real-world appreciation to someone.

- Write a gratitude journal or list. This helps retrain your brain to notice things to be appreciative and grateful for.

- Give plant cuttings to people as a token of your appreciation. This is a beautiful gesture, and you will get double the points if you give new plants to other witches!

- If you think of something you appreciate, like a particular poem or social media post or the way your barista always goes above and beyond, tell them! Reflect on these moments while meditating with an amethyst crystal for an added witchy boost.

CHAPTER 6

Be Soulful

We've touched on it many times throughout this book, but one of the biggest keys to unlocking joy and truly stepping into your magic is to move in a state of flow and alignment with your spirit. No more playing small or taking action that isn't backed by your belief systems. No more clinging to limiting paradigms that don't nourish your soul, when what you need to be doing is leaning into your hunger to live a deliciously free life. You must commit to yourself, to your spirit, and to cultivating a life that is magically empowered in order to thrive.

In this chapter, you will practice being the magic you want to see in the world! Hold fast in your power as a spiritually connected person who is guided by joy and consciously deciding to relentlessly pursue happiness through mindset and action. We need to start giving our own personal joy more space on the priority list. You will open up to the big, magical joy that comes from relieving yourself of the pressures to live in some prescribed way, and move toward living in a way that feels right to *you*. The path of the witch may still be a road that some struggle to understand, but the beautiful thing about it is that those who walk it find a deep and meaningful form of happiness with a solid foundation in both mindset and action. It's time to live in a way that is soulful and nurture the sparks of magic that lie in the corners of your everyday life.

Stay in Your Magic, Keep in Your Power

Magic can help you feel powerful, but there can be a big difference between the way you feel post-ritual and the way you feel as you're going through your mundane life. The feeling of connectedness and otherworldly magic can get lost in the shuffle sometimes when the day-to-day chaos starts piling up, leaving you feeling zapped and depleted.

No more!

Cultivating a magical life can be the antidote to feeling pressed by the mundane and disconnected from your power. This is the big secret of the craft: It allows you to keep perspective of the fact that you are infinitely more powerful than you are led to believe, through mindset, will, and intentionally choosing your healing and happiness over and over again. Although adult human life can feel dreadfully confusing and lonely, for the witch this solitude is a blessing—an opportunity for you to work on your growth and step into your power.

There are always going to be things that come along and trip you up on the route to happiness. It is your job to make calming the chaos just as important a part of your priority list as any other mundane task. Joy isn't the prize that comes from everything going right in your life; it is something that you need to make space for and cultivate yourself, even when it feels impossible (especially then!). Humans naturally want to be in a state of happiness and ease, and by shifting your mindset and prioritizing your wellness you will find yourself closer to that goal. Sometimes it's just as simple as not dwelling on the madness playing out around you, instead turning your attention to your visualizations and your hopes and reminding yourself of your personal power.

Although witchcraft has no rules, and your spiritual practices are likely to ebb and flow through time, there is big healing power in remaining tapped in to your mystical side as a way of self-care. The feelings of empowerment that magic gives you can be a useful tool for getting through life, making strengthening these connections a worthy priority in times of overwhelm. It doesn't take much to nurture this connection, either. Sometimes all it takes is some intention setting, some challenging of limiting beliefs, and a relentless commitment to realigning your vibe.

There is so much more to life than this mundane chaos. Make an intentional choice to stay in your power, remind yourself of it, and fully own the implications. You *are* magic, and your life is the spell you are casting on the world! Make every day drip with enchantment, and lean into your magic as a source of light to illuminate the path forward.

You are not meant to simply be alive; you are meant to truly thrive! You are an infinitely powerful and magical creature—don't ever underestimate your ability to shift, to overcome, and to build a juicy-delicious life filled with empowered, connected joy.

A Mirror Dedication Ritual

The following ritual is a simple one, using just a mirror and your favorite scents and sounds to realign and make a commitment to yourself to stay in your magic.

1. Light some candles and put on some soothing instrumental music.

2. Get cozy with a mirror that is large enough to see your face and to place both your hands on.

3. Cleanse yourself and your mirror, and ground your energy by deep breathing in through your nose and out through your mouth as you imagine that you are pulling calming, centered energy up through your feet and exhaling any stress or anxious BS through your mouth.

4. Place both hands on the mirror so you are essentially holding hands with your reflection. Gaze into your own eyes and state out loud your commitment to yourself and your magic. It can be really meaningful to make up your commitment wording based on your own particular beliefs and hang-ups when it comes to your own mysticism, but an example would be: "I choose to see your magic and to support your growth as a magical being. I release any hang-ups and limitations that are standing in the way of becoming the spiritually empowered witch that I am meant to be. I commit to my magic and to stepping fully into my power."

5. Keep gazing into your eyes and repeating your commitment until you begin feeling strong in your conviction and a little bit excited (it should feel like a "buzzing" sensation in your body). Once this happens, state your commitment once more.

6. Blow out your candles, and rest. If anything came up that you need to work through in order to release it, have a little freewriting session in your journal.

Treat Your Home As a Sacred Space

One of the most compelling aspects of the craft is animism. There is a very special kind of connected magic in treating your life and the things in it as fluid and alive, things you can build a relationship *with*. In nurturing these relationships, you get to reap the benefits, but as with most things, the happiness you get back is dependent on the energy you put in. Take, for instance, your home. Your home is meant to be your sanctuary and escape from the world at large—how are you treating it?

Mundane and energetic cleansing of the home space is a routine part of most witches' practice. This is done because it is important to have a space that's yours, where you can feel safe, comfortable, and protected. While schools, workplaces, and the like are spaces that you need to work with despite not having control over the details, your home space (or bedroom in the case of shared living arrangements) can be a place where you can exercise your will over their aesthetic presentation and energetics.

This is your sacred space—your safe haven from the wildly unpredictable outside world! The magic of place and setting is very subtle, but it is powerful when you can tap in to what it has to offer. People typically don't second-guess the idea of magical spaces that are found out in nature (chances are good you probably have one in mind while reading this!), but all too often the sacred magic and "aliveness" of the home and other personal spaces are overlooked only because they make up part of the mundane fabric of the everyday world. In directing yourself to work *with* these energies in a reciprocal way, you can enrich your life and, by extension, your happiness.

The pace of life can be overwhelming, and in the grips of depression or just general fatigue from being a person, your spaces can become neglected, turning into another source of stress and obligation. It can be a really difficult cycle to break (boy, do I know it!), but in recognizing that your home has a spirit deserving of nurturing, you can find yourself more magically connected and happier in general by having a safe space that's tended with your loving energy. This space is where you can retreat from the chaos of the outside world and just *be*, to vibe in your magic and to realign and recharge your spirit.

Approach your home as a magical space and, in return, watch it support you as a magical being! A large part of your practice will likely take place in the home, so treat it as if it's an integral part of your spiritual universe (because it *is*!). Speak aloud to it, show gratitude for it, and most importantly, treat it respectfully and make the care of it a priority.

A Simmer Pot for Positive Energy

The following is an activity to diffuse positive magic into the air of your home.

Materials

- ½ large grapefruit
- 2 sprigs dried rosemary
- 1 sprig dried thyme

- 1 tablespoon dried lavender buds

- 1 tablespoon dried rose petals

- A big pinch cedar (leaves from the branches, or wood chips)

- 6 drops lemon essential oil

- 6 drops peppermint essential oil

Instructions

1. Place all ingredients in a large pot of water. Heat to a boil, then simmer, allowing the fragrance of the herbs, fruit, and oils to fill your space.

2. Open the windows to freshen the energy and get the air flowing.

3. Sing, dance, or play upbeat music to fill the space up with uplifting joy and good positive energy!

Don't Be Afraid to Lose Your Mind

As a secular witch and generally science-minded person, I often feel my inner critic looking at me banging on about energies and consciousness in abject horror. My skepticism is much less a denial of the mystic and more a defense mechanism that I adapted in reaction to challenges with mental health and impaired perception. I find myself on high alert when it comes to speaking freely about my innermost mystical tendencies and personal beliefs.

This is actually a very valid and normal thing. Modern society downplays anything that it deems irrational, and there is this subliminal message that if you are somehow outside the norm of what's considered prevailing thought, then you are an outsider, or some sort of delusional person. This is an interesting occurrence when you consider that historically it was the mystics who held a great place of status in society (and in some cultures around the world, this continues to be the case). But science and spirituality don't have to be at odds at all, and an integration of both can open up the human experience in ways that will leave you better off as a whole.

As a being infused with a unique spirit, you are meant to be a spiritual creature, and denying this leads you to diminished returns in terms of happiness. This is the source of so much of that longing, that deep ache you may feel that you don't belong, that craving for more that can lead people to identify too strongly with ideologies or things like their own mental illnesses. What you are is a multidimensional being who is living in the illusion of a three-dimensional existence. You are so much bigger and harder to define than a label or even a series of labels. It isn't you, your beliefs, or your dreams that are the problem, however: It's the culture at large that benefits from keeping you unaware of your magic, of your spark that has the power to light up the world and show you the way!

The world desperately needs more people who are connected to nature and leading with heart. It needs those who are willing to declare comfort with the unknown, willing to chase expansion and tune in to the frequency of unlimited potential. This illusion that you as an individual are powerless or somehow not good enough if your beliefs aren't within the accepted norm is bullshit of the highest order! You are powerful. You are valid. And awakening to this will lead to more people finding the courage to embody their values, live in harmony, and be willing to step up in alignment with their hearts and spirits. This is what the world needs, and if doing so makes you a weirdo, then darling, let's be outcasts together!

Living your happiest magical life all starts with the answer to this question: How would you show up to your life if you had never known fear? Hurdle over your fears and get comfortable with being swept up in the tides of life and challenged as a way to connect with spirit.

Shadow Work Prompts to Embrace Your Inner Mystic

The following prompts are meant to help you tease out your relationship with your own mysticism. Feel free to approach these in any order you choose. You may answer them chrono-logically or pick out the ones that stand out for you as poten-tially personally relevant.

1. How do you view spirituality? Does it feel safe?

2. As you were growing up, what were some of the messages you got about spirituality and mysticism? Think of as many examples as you can (they can be from your family and friends or more general, such as the messages from TV and films).

3. Imagine your "Witch Self." This is the version of you who has no qualms stepping into their power as a mystical, spiritual being. Write out what this version of you is like: How do they act? How do they carry themselves? How do they look and feel?

4. As you build on this idea of your Witch Self, explore the areas where this version of you might have blind spots. What can you learn from this?

5. Draw or sketch your Witch Self. Much like you can build a vision of your higher self in order to get familiar with this aspect of yourself, you can bring to life the more mystical aspects of yourself that you are encouraged to suppress in a logic-based world. Spend some time exploring this Witch Self, then integrate what you can learn from this aspect of yourself to become a more balanced and whole person.

Call In the Life You Want

While growing up, most of us went to schools that allowed us to learn and socialize with our peers. We learned to sit nicely and take turns, to show our work, and to raise our hands to speak. Due to the unfiltered nature of children, we learned quickly how to fit in and what happens if we don't. We gained an education beyond the learning, a molding and shaping of what it means to be a *socially acceptable person*. While this isn't a totally bad thing (we evolved to be prosocial in groups, which had selective advantage), it can leave many of us struggling to find ourselves and pull that self out once we're thrust into the grown world.

As you have gotten older, you may have found yourself desperately digging to find who you really are underneath the programming. Although to outsiders this journey of discovery can be jarring, it's an important return to self as you start asking questions like: "Who am I really? What are my values? How am I showing up to my life, and does it feel authentic to me? What do I *truly* want?" This process is much like a blossoming, as you take back the reins of your life and choose to live more fully on your own terms, even if you haven't fully figured out what those terms are yet.

This is the beautiful, messy work of finding your spark again!

The important thing to remember is that you *are* the magic, and your life is the spell! A unique concoction created from your experiences, beliefs, and values—the soulful blend that makes you who you are. Whenever you betray your desires and values in order to conform or please, you are pledging allegiance to the wrong things. It is your duty to yourself and to your happiness and wellness to abandon this idea that you need to live by anybody else's terms. As long as you do no harm, your life is your own and your energy and focus would be best spent going hard for the things that are important to you and your spirit. This not only uplifts you on an individual level but also inspires those around you as you get to shine in the full brilliance of who you *truly* are.

You only have one amazing life; spend it in full momentum, chasing the things you want and living in alignment with your truth. You must make a commitment to yourself to no longer be available for scraps, spending your precious energy trying to fit into dreams and norms that are not your own.

Call in the life you want!

Your life and your happiness are enhanced by living on your own terms. So figure out what that is; define your goals and desires, and don't settle for anything less than a full steam ahead energy in order to get there! Cast a spell on the world that is entirely your own.

A Defining Your Desires Activity

This activity is meant to engage your personal creativity to define your desires, which helps you gain clarity for the life you want to call in. Although words like "definition" and "clarity" can bring to mind some degree of dry logic, this activity is to help you lean into the chaos and creativity that can help you envision the things you want to see! This mood board can be done in hard copy with poster board, magazine cutouts, photos, and doodles, or it can be done digitally as a photo grid, collage, or *Pinterest* board. Whichever method you choose, the important thing is to have it be easily accessible and visible.

To create the board, collect images that represent the things you want to see in your life. These images can be based on a vibe (having a particular aesthetic appeal), tangible things you want to see in your life, activities (such as frolicking on a beach or tending to a garden—you do you!), or a bucket list or goal, or they can simply be photos that are symbolic of...well, anything, really! The less focus you put on doing this "correctly," the more impact it will have. You are essentially creating a mood board for the type of life you want and the type of person you want to be in order to make the shift to get there.

Every day, spend up to five minutes gazing at your mood board as you hold a black obsidian crystal or clear quartz. When you have done this, pop the crystal in your pocket or a bag you carry with you daily (a bra works too!) so that it will be there with you as you move through life, showing up as the most authentic you possible!

Cultivate Hope and Expect Miracles

Immersed in this cosmic soup of what-the-fuck-ery, you may find yourself struggling to find solid ground when it comes to things that are or are not within your control. It can feel as if circumstances are imposed upon you, and sometimes the weight of your perceived powerlessness is simply too heavy to bear. However, for the witch, there is always a door left open for miracles, whether it be through cosmic intervention or a reframing of possibilities. There is always room for hope—a very special form of resistance when the walls feel as if they are closing in on you.

Hope can be a trigger for many, causing visceral reactions in either positive or negative directions. For some, hope is seen as pure folly and a bypassing of very real issues. For others, hope is the ultimate goal—barriers and unjust realities be damned! The concept of hope can poke at your wounds in unexpected ways because it reveals important things about your fundamental belief systems about life, suffering, and destiny. For some, hope can be seen as a foolish bypassing of very real hardships, while for others, hope is the great medicine to help push through hard times. While you don't want to ignore reality or dismiss a true difficulty, you can respect hardship while still cultivating hope that the future will be brighter. Hope has the power to propel your evolution without the aid of a road map, a wandering in the darkness that is common for witches and mystics alike.

Simply put, hope is the ability to look beyond the reality you're dealt and believe that there is something better to be had. To hold space for hope is to plant tiny seeds of light that can illuminate even the blackest darkness. There is big magic in hope, especially in the face of hardship and adversity. After all, this is the fodder for those beloved feel-good stories; tales of triumphs and overcoming obstacles are compelling because you can feel the medicine that comes with envisioning brighter days ahead. Deep down inside, there's a spark in everyone that longs to look past the limitations of what's being served up and to dream of something better. How you choose to stoke those embers is then up to you!

Choose hope as you would choose happy. They feed each other, forming an ecosystem in your mindset that is fertile ground for nurturing your dreams. What a shame it is to give up hope; to do so is to put blinders on that would have you cut off from unexpected blessings. To give up hope is also to give up your power, because if you believe that you have none or that your actions don't matter, you're more apt to roll over, binding yourself.

No more of that shit!

Good things can happen to you and *likely will*. If you believe it, you may be more apt to see opportunities right in front of your face. Shift the perspective that life just happens, expect the unexpected, and tend to those embers of hope until their flames can wrap you up in their warmth.

After all, the path of the witch is one that is comfortable in the darkness, guided by spirit and by a firm belief that if you want something to happen, you do it yourself! Let hope light your way and unleash the happiness that can come with such a brazen approach toward life.

A Spell for Opening the Road to Hope

This spell acts as a psychological prompt to yourself and a message to the Universe that you are ready for the doors of hope to be thrown open! Use it to call in some powerful shifts.

Materials

- A yellow candle

- A nail or thumbtack

- A candleholder (a small cube holder used for chime candles works best for this)

- A wide bowl or dish

- Some fresh flower petals (I love dandelions for this because they are so bright and cheerful, and as one of the first flowers of spring, they scream big hopeful energy!)

- A key-shaped charm or actual key

Instructions

1. Take your candle and carve the word "HOPE" into the side with the nail or thumbtack. Place the candle in the candleholder.

2. Place your candle in the center of your bowl or dish. Surround the candle with the fresh petals, and let the sight of the petals fill you with hope and joy. Take the time to be mindfully present as you do this, paying close attention to their scent, the way they look as they scatter, and how they feel in your fingers.

3. Light your candle.

4. Take your key and swirl it around your candle nine times, moving clockwise. State out loud your intent to have the doors of hope become available and visible for you.

5. Now press the key gently on each of your eyelids for a moment, as well as over your third eye area in the center of your forehead.

6. Repeat steps 4 and 5 daily for up to nine days, replacing the flowers when they begin to wilt.

Open Up to Spirit

Stepping into your power as a witch is not easy territory. It's an intentional movement outside the lines that are drawn for you. It's a rejection of collective norms and limiting beliefs, and a devotion to living in alignment with realities that have not yet presented themselves. For the faint of heart or eager to please, it can be immensely uncomfortable, but the overall returns when it comes to happiness make it worth the work.

This modern era is dominated by a paradigm that tends to diminish the spiritual. It's often considered unnecessary and even mocked and ridiculed. However, the need to be spiritual could very well be the missing link in reconnecting people to their happiness and power. Of course, by stepping up and embracing that as a part of your life, you open yourself up to possible scrutiny, which is an understandably hard position to be in.

That being said, it's worth the potential side-eye.

The Universe is vast, and your very existence is just one tiny particle in the drops in the bucket of strange mysteries. Even as a secular witch myself, I have found immense joy in embracing the fact that humans don't know everything, nor are they entitled to. By opening up to spirit and allowing yourself to walk the line between the magic and the mundane with zero fucks given to how other people perceive it, you are making yourself open and available to beautiful magic and strong, empowered guidance.

Throughout human history, channeling, scrying, living in alignment with the cosmos, and embracing superstition have been fundamental parts of life. Although these things have become fringe interests in the modern context, opening yourself up in a spiritual way doesn't necessarily have to be in opposition to the prevailing paradigm of logic and science. In fact, they can complement one another in beautiful ways, allowing you to widen the bandwidth of this human experience in a way that can fill you with true magical joy. Both can color your understanding of the world and your life. My own personal approach to the craft has always been rooted in personal empowerment—I refuse to believe in a powerless existence. Although I consider myself skeptical almost to a fault, I still allow myself to wander the realm of the spiritual, stoking the embers of spirituality that lie within to benefit from their warmth.

Everyone has the ability to tap in to guidance that's beyond regular brain chatter—if they take the time to listen and be still. Whether you access that guidance through cards, by staring into flames or bowls of dark water, or by any other means isn't the point. The point is that by opening yourself up to receive understanding and nuggets of wisdom that may ordinarily be hidden, you are able to live in a way that is less dictated by others and more guided by personal truth and well-being. Guidance is guidance and help is help, and I for one will take whatever I can get to make this walk of life easier. How others choose to perceive me is not my concern, but my happiness and wellness most certainly are!

A Channeling Exercise

The following exercise can help you open up to spirit. It's important to note that your worldview doesn't matter in this practice. Whether you believe you are channeling from a divine source, from the self, or from something else entirely is beside the point. What matters is that you are channeling something beyond the mundane.

1. Set the mood with any scents or music that you prefer.

2. Begin by cleansing yourself and your space, lighting a purple candle, and setting the intention to open up to spirit. Sipping tea made with herbs like mugwort can also aid in this process by allowing you to slip into a dreamy and open state.

3. Begin your channeling practice.*

*There are many ways to channel with different results—for instance, I channel in a creative sense when writing, painting, or dancing. Some people channel musically, allowing songs or notes to move through them. Still others may write out the things they are channeling, the purpose being to glean some knowledge or perhaps aid in making decisions. An important distinction to make before you start is this: Are you channeling to gain anything in particular (for example, recording your results or using them to guide you), or are you simply opening up for the experience of doing so itself (for instance, channeling songs or dance with no recording in place to capture these moments)? As with most aspects of the craft, clear intent is key.

*When channeling, it is important to get to that magical zone that is so important for spellwork and spiritual pursuits such as scrying. The space where it feels as if you fully have your feet planted "somewhere else," no longer fully enveloped in the mundane experience. As you vibe in this space, allow yourself to freely move with impulse. For example, if you are writing, then just write whatever chooses to come *through* you. If you are painting, allow your hands to move in the way that they choose. If you are speaking out loud, using your voice and words as the channel, then let your mouth move and allow spirit to take you over. This is where inhibitions and silly fears and self-conscious inclinations go to die. Channeling is a merging of worlds, and it requires a transcendence and openness of spirit to be the prevailing priority.

Shine Bright As a Beacon

The witch is an archetype that has captivated the human collective for ages. There is something truly compelling about a person who chooses to be aligned with spirit, discarding the shackles of conformity and dancing the line between worlds, free of mundane limitations. Whether positive or negative in the eye of the beholder, the witch's dedication to themselves, to nature, and to living their truth fully shines bright in a way that can instill inspiration—or small-minded fear.

On this adventure to uncover your joy through the craft, you need to keep front and center in your awareness the understanding that you are only here for a limited time, and that time should not be wasted trying to stay small for the comfort of others. One of the greatest illusions you face in this world is that you are obligated to fit in—that this is a prerequisite for being accepted, happy, and loved. This couldn't be further from the truth.

Consider the possibility that you are here to inspire, to awaken, to disrupt!

This paradigm of fitting in as the way to happiness is shifting, and people are experiencing the growing pains that come with it. You may already know that keeping up with the Joneses is a limiting belief, and when scrolling online, you're sure to find countless memes about living your truth loudly....But how many people are ready to embrace the discomfort of what living your truth actually means in action? You need to adjust, correct your course, and conjure up the courage to stand for yourself in a way that acts as a beacon for others to do the same. And by light, I don't mean the positive-vibes-only crap that's simply an over-correction in the *other* direction of happiness. What I'm talking about is the spark of truth: the flickering flame of wild, untamed joy that comes with living in alignment with your soul. This is the example, the lighthouse to lead others in stepping up and doing the same.

This joy you feel when you are with your people is the deep alignment that comes when you feel seen and understood. For the witch, this joy can be sourced not only by the companionship of like-minded others, but by deepening your relationship to yourself. The light you hold is your guide in the often-dark chaos of the world, yet it can also act as a beacon for others to release their chains and walk forward confidently in their own groove. When seeing a person reject people-pleasing in favor of living their wild, authentic truth, you see that the world still spins! The sun still rises! And that person who dares to move in line with their truth feasts at the table of joy.

So step up, be brave, and be a shining example of what can happen if you unleash your freest self and indulge in joy. Light the way for others to kindle this spark too.

A Talisman for Letting Your Light Shine

This activity will guide you in making a talisman you can wear to become magically empowered to bravely show up as your brightest, most authentic self.

Materials

- Cleansing tools of your choice

- A crystal or item of jewelry that you can wear or carry on your person day to day

Instructions

1. Begin by cleansing your space and setting up the space for magic.

2. Sit and take a few deep, grounding breaths in through your nose and out through your mouth. Focus your awareness on the energy within your body. Try to raise and direct your energy up through your arms and into your palms.

3. Place your open hands above your item and visualize your energy as radiating light that flows from your palms and into the object.

4. Repeat a chant or affirmation of intent—something like, "Let this talisman grant me the power to shine so bright it cuts through the darkness and acts as a beacon for others to unleash their sparkle. Let it give me bravery and courage to show up in my brightest form." Repeat until you begin to feel your energy waning.

5. Thank your talisman for the work you are about to do with its help, and place it on you while you look into a mirror, anchoring its link to you.

Tend to Your Magical Garden

Your magic is like your dreams: It should be treated as a part of your spiritual garden, tended to and nourished. Even as a secular witch, I understand my magic to be a living, breathing thing that I am responsible for nurturing and that, if nurtured correctly, it will nurture me back. The difficult work of staying in your magic is to allow it to be a dynamic thing. Indeed, what worked for you at one point may not necessarily at another, and your relationship with it may ebb and flow as your other relationships do. This is absolutely a normal and good thing.

The work of stepping into your power and trying to cultivate a delicious and joyful life is ongoing and ever-shifting. It should not be so much a set of rules or rigid attitudes toward the world as it is a constant checking in with yourself about how you feel, what your values are, and what kind of energy you feel is best to cultivate at any given moment. Sometimes your life calls for you to be steady in your magic, while other times it requires you to place your energies elsewhere. The truly important part is to ensure that the embers stay warm through every stage of life so that you can benefit from their warmth whenever needed.

Although every witch's practice looks different, many already know the specific things that open them up and brighten their spirits. Once you have identified what these things are for you, you would be wise to incorporate them into your world on a regular basis. However, remember to make note when something no longer fills you up. This is why the most important aspect of your practice should be a connection and knowledge of the self and a willingness to shake shit up if you need it to be shaken!

Your happiness is also like your magic: a beautiful part of your inner garden that needs to be tended to in a deliberate and intentional way. Indeed, your magic, your happiness, and your willingness to be true to your spirit all feed into each other and form a beautiful ecosystem of vibing and thriving. You must make a deep relationship with this garden, cultivating it, weeding it, feeding it, and taking the time to appreciate the things that bloom in it. And, as with all things in life, there must be balance between the growth and decay in your garden. Sometimes you may water it with your tears and fertilize it with the decaying matter of the things you thought you wanted but have chosen to let die. Healing is not linear or a pretty thing worthy of *Instagram*. It is the churning of the wheel of fortune and the necessity of the highs and lows, of new joys blooming and past joys withering, in order for balance to reign.

So when calling in magic to cultivate more happiness, remember that this is a lifestyle and not just a plan you set in motion. Consistently nurture it well.

A Poppet to Nurture Your Magical Spirit

A poppet is a little magical doll that typically represents a person or an aspect of the self. Poppets can be used in a variety of ways in witchcraft. In this activity, your poppet will act as an analog for your spiritual side. Nurture it accordingly!

Materials

- A large piece of felt or thick fabric
- A pen or pencil
- Scissors
- A needle and some thread
- A few cotton balls (enough to flesh out poppet)
- A pinch dried mugwort
- Some strands of your hair
- A small labradorite stone

Instructions

1. Fold your felt or fabric in half and draw the shape of a person on one half.

2. While it's folded, cut out the outline of the person, so you are left with two person-shaped pieces.

3. Stack the pieces and sew around the edges to make your poppet. Leave a gap at the head large enough to fit the other materials.

4. Stuff your poppet with the cotton balls, dried mugwort, strands of hair, and labradorite crystal. Sew up the gap.

5. This poppet is to represent your mystical side. Take care of it, speak to it, and leave it under your pillow. When you are finding that your magic feels as if it is waning, ask the poppet what it needs or place it on your altar. This is a physical representation of your magical spirit—treat it well and let this be an interactive process!

INDEX

ABOUT THE AUTHOR

Mandi Em is a humorist, author, and chaotic wellness witch. She's the author of *Witchcraft Therapy*, and she shares funny, approachable self-help guidance on her blog and social channels for *Healing for Hot Messes* and resources for nonreligious witches over at *The Secular Witch*. Her writing has been featured in *The New York Times*, *HuffPost*, *SheKnows*, *Refinery29*, *McSweeney's*, and more. She and her husband are born-again hippies raising their three children in beautiful Vernon, British Columbia, Canada.